MW00938563

On Wings of Hope

Leading Lily Home

To Joanna ~ a beautiful soul,
May this true story bring you
comfort and peace.
abundant blessings,
Cynthia

Cynthia Lynch Bischoff, PhD

iUniverse

ON WINGS OF HOPE
LEADING LILY HOME

iUniverse books may be ordered through booksellers or by contacting:

iUniverse
1663 Liberty Drive
Bloomington, IN 47403
www.iuniverse.com
844-349-9409

ISBN: 978-1-5320-8144-6 (sc)
ISBN: 978-1-5320-8146-0 (hc)
ISBN: 978-1-5320-8145-3 (e)

Library of Congress Control Number: 2019912783

Print information available on the last page.

iUniverse rev. date: 12/18/2019

For Lily,
a beautiful soul who taught me so much.

Contents

A Note to the Reader

This book is based on a true story. Some names and identifying details of individuals, locations, and situations in the book have been changed to protect privacy.

Preface

Have you ever wondered about the universe, your purpose here on earth, or what might await you in the afterlife?

I have worked as an international life coach, motivational speaker, and healing practitioner for more than twenty years. My passion is to assist others in finding greater meaning in their lives. Over the years, hundreds of clients have asked me to write a book that would summarize my teachings based on my wisdom and life lessons.

As I reflected on the message I could offer, I realized that none of my work has been as profound as that which I experienced with a dear client, Lily, who passed away from breast cancer at a young age. Our transformational work together weaves the basis of my overall understanding of life, my Heartliving principles, and my desire to bring hope and transcendence to all who suffer.

I believe that every experience in our lives is important and valuable. Every moment has been essential to our growth as spiritual beings. In fact, it is in all the events of our lives, both good and bad, that we can ultimately find true meaning.

My own life is a case in point. Prior to becoming a life coach, I was a faculty administrator at a university and a single mother of two young children. In both my work and home life, my world was overflowing with pressure and heavy responsibilities. There was always more to do than was possible, and achieving balance in my life felt like a goal but never a real possibility. Despite the challenges,

I still believed that each of us comes into the world to be the best version of ourselves.

During this demanding time in my life, a turning point occurred in 1997. I took a life-changing trip to Croatia during the aftermath of the Bosnian War to connect with other cultures who were joining to pray for world peace. Even though my life was incredibly busy with responsibilities that were hard to delegate, I knew this was an opportunity that I needed to take. I could step out of my current lifestyle and do some much-needed soul-searching, and I had so many questions: *What am I doing with my life? Why am I here? What contribution could I be making?*

On a very important evening in Bosnia, I was one of thousands participating in a vigil for peace in Medjugorje. The site of our gathering was a famous church there, and it was so packed that every inch of space was taken with a person kneeling or standing. People from more than eighteen countries had gathered. As I knelt on the marble floor in the back of the church, the leader asked us to pray.

While people of many cultures joined hands, words were spoken in different languages. I closed my eyes, and amid the dissonance of sound, an inspiring vision came to me of an old woman wearing a dark cloak. I could not see her face. Her shoulders were bent, and from the opening in the front of her cloak, I could see that she had a diversely colored, multilayered heart from which people were leaping. They were of all nationalities and emotions—old, young, angry, joyful—all leaping from the old woman's heart. It was an incredibly powerful image that I will never forget. While the meaning of this vision was not readily apparent to me, I knew that it would ultimately be life changing.

Upon returning home, I continued my university work, all the time questioning my life's mission. I spent moments each day meditating on the heart vision. I researched the heart and discovered the concept of "heart consciousness." I was inspired by the works of Dr. Dean Ornish and the HeartMath Institute, among others. Repeatedly, the research suggested that the heart has a unique intelligence unto itself. I understood that when people accessed their heart intelligence, they were able to achieve greater life balance.

By chance, I discovered a quote by Henry David Thoreau: "The cost of a thing is the amount of life you have to exchange for it, either now or in the long run." I questioned my life and how I was spending my energy. Within a year, I knew that I would leave my university position and that my new work would include helping others express themselves authentically in a safe, healing environment. Deep down, I felt that I had to surrender to a consciousness greater than I. I knew I was birthing a new self.

Excited about the possibilities for helping myself and others transform, I enrolled in certification programs both in the US and abroad to learn energy-based healing methods, such as hypnotherapy, transformative psychology, and metaphysics—all of which I coupled with my business and university background.

In 1998, I created Heartliving, a business dedicated to empowering others to lead healthier, happier lives. My unique curriculum was grounded in both business and intuitive principles. I designed my heart logo from my vision in Bosnia, and more than twenty-one years later, I continue my mission to guide others to greater life meaning and a deeper understanding of themselves.

Heartliving has spanned the US, Japan, and Europe, and to date, thousands have become clients of Heartliving consciousness through seminars, products, and individual work.

It is my desire that *On Wings of Hope: Leading Lily Home* will inspire you to become the best version of yourself so that, like Lily, you may find meaning and peace in our world.

Acknowledgments

First, I wish to thank my Heartliving community in the US and abroad who have trusted me to help them, who have believed in this work, and who have been there for me every step of the way. So many amazing people to thank, so many generous and loving hearts. I believe that together we can change the world, and in fact, I know we've already begun. Thank you so much, my dear heart family.

Thank you to the incredible, hardworking team at iUniverse for taking on this project, for handling so many details and offering helpful suggestions, and for their patience, expertise, and desire to promote this work globally.

Special thanks to my loving family, especially my dear mother, Dolores Morgan Lynch, and my late father, John Stephen Lynch Jr., who always encouraged me to love and respect others and to lend my heart to those in need. They are the forerunners of my Heartliving creation.

Thank you to my dear children—to my daughter, Courtney Frazer; to my son and daughter-in-law, Matthew and Candice Frazer; and to my beautiful grandchildren, Zachary and Evelyn. I'm so grateful that I am your mother and Mimi! It is the greatest honor of my life.

To a very special man in my life, David Jordan, I have the sincerest gratitude. You encouraged me to write this book, sat with me countless hours as I wrote and read passages and asked for feedback, offered support and expert advice, and more than that, you were always there encouraging me to believe in myself and in the value of *On Wings of Hope: Leading Lily Home*. Your generous support and love mean the world to me.

Finally, to Lily's beautiful family, thank you for allowing me to be present with Lily at her passing, and most of all, to Lily herself, I offer you the greatest gratitude for sharing your life with me and for being such an amazing teacher.

"I Am Here, Lily."

I keep a faithful watch over Lily as her spirit floats gently between worlds. Candles flicker ever so softly, illuminating family pictures of happier times, while alabaster angels, shimmering necklaces, and personal treasures adorn the bedroom. The plaque I gave Lily a month ago is next to her grandmother's picture on the nightstand. A heart-shaped locket hangs from her bedpost. It is open, containing a picture of her mother, who smiles sweetly.

Lily lies in acceptance, surrendered in the center of her four-poster bed. Floor-length taffeta curtains line the windows on either side. Her blonde hair is brushed back from her face. Her skin has gone pale, and her lips dry. She no longer opens her intense blue eyes. I reflect on whether Lily knew that this room she called her sanctuary would be her last place on earth.

A tapestry of Archangel Gabriel hangs on the wall above her bed. The angel's face and wings are woven intricately into the cloth, the careful handiwork of a European artist. Rich colors of navy and rose highlight the angel's form. It appears both feminine and masculine with soft, flowing robes and large, strong wings, genderless, a combination of elements both human and divine.

Archangel Gabriel's name, Lily told me, means "God is my strength." This angel is the messenger, the deliverer of souls from their fears, an angel she prayed to and felt the presence of many times. Lily placed the tapestry above the head of her bed to remind her to open her heart, to cleanse her spirit, and to connect with all that would come to be.

It is now nearing midnight, and I am grateful that a new nurse, who introduces herself as Helena, has arrived. We learn that she has worked in hospice[1] for years. She appears to be in her early sixties. Her light pink scrubs are well pressed, her nurse's shoes white and clean, and her jewelry and makeup minimal. Her olive skin and hazel eyes are framed by her short, dark hair. Helena has a calm and gentle demeanor.

After assessing Lily's vitals and hearing her labored breathing, she removes the loud oxygen machine next to Lily's bed, telling us that she no longer needs it. We welcome the sudden silence.

"Cynthia?" she whispers to me. "Tell me about Lily. What is important to her?"

My lips quiver as I look down and choose my words carefully. "Lily loves nature and plants and animals. She loves her family." I pause. "She has such a big heart."

Helena suggests that I bring a few of Lily's plants from the living room into the bedroom as well as family pictures that might fit on the nightstands. I gather a few items, placing a prayer plant on the nightstand next to a picture of her grandmother. Together, we create a display of love.

Helena gently pulls the comforter up, exposing Lily's feet. She rubs her patient's feet with lotion until the smell of roses fills the air. She glances at me. "Do you have any soft music that might soothe her?" I put on a familiar flute instrumental, one that I know Lily would recognize. This nurse is a midwife of her soul, I realize.

---

[1] "End of Life: What Are Palliative Care and Hospice Care?" NIH > National Institute on Aging, US Department of Health and Human Services, accessed March 17, 2019, https://www.nia.nih.gov/health/what-are-palliative-care-and-hospice-care#hospice.

Lily's brother, Andrew, and I pull up chairs and are now on each side of the foot of her bed. Lily once described Andrew to me as a gentle giant—tall and broad shouldered with a round face, sandy hair, and deeply set eyes. Andrew is older than Lily but doesn't look his age of forty-six years; nor does Lily look forty-three.

Helena sits near the bed and whispers softly to Lily's brother and me that Lily may leave us this very night. "But how does one truly know God's plan?" she admits. We exchange glances and pull our chairs closer to the bed.

Andrew is clearly upset and has spoken little. I can tell as he looks down at his hands, his feelings are just under the surface. His anxiety is palpable. Their sister, Colette, has gone into the living room to rest on the couch, having been up for hours attending to Lily's every need. Andrew is to awaken her if it appears time for Lily to pass.

Lily's hair is braided to one side, and although she is bedridden, she is not wearing a gown but rather her favorite long purple dress. It is as though the day nurse who dressed her believed she might get up and join us.

In contrast, and as though indifferent to these sacred moments, Lily's calico cat scratches on the floor in the corner, staring at us from time to time, rudely clawing the designer silk scarf that I gave Lily from my travels only weeks ago. On it are sewn two angels holding hands, floating above the world, free of pain and suffering. Something I wished for her.

Suddenly, the antique clock on the mantel chimes midnight. I glance to see a large iron peacock, perfectly centered on the mantel, feathered eyes staring at me, as though it knew all along this moment would come.

I clasp my hands over my chest, and I focus on Lily, sending her a message from my heart: *I'm here, Lily. Just as I promised you. I will not leave your side. Nothing is more important than this moment. Nothing is more important.*

It is a cold December night, and my world is quiet as I lie awake in bed, huddled under the blankets, peering into the darkness. Several days have passed, and Lily's family is making arrangements for the funeral.

My mind wanders often to those last few days before she passed when we talked about so many things—where she was going, who would come for her, what it would be like. She told me she was ready.

I want her to know that I was watching over her as she gently slipped away. As her spirit left her body, I noticed the plaque engraved with the words, "A little birdie told me you are so brave." Just as I had hoped, I knew her grandmother had come to take her home.

I miss her so much. During times like tonight, while waiting for the early-morning light, I think of her. Just several days before she passed, Lily lost her vision, and I would read the cards to her that came in daily, describing the pictures. She told me that her dog that had passed years before was playing about now in the room, waiting for her.

"Will I go today?" she had asked. I reminded her that it had taken forty-three years to get her to this day. The right day, we decided, would be in perfect order and divine timing. It was so hard to watch her waiting in between worlds.

I remember the first day she walked through my office door, so vulnerable and so ready to heal. I remember her gentleness as we surmised in our classes what life was all about here on the earth plane and what the other side might be like in all its dimensions. When someone would share their deepest feelings, the tears would well in her eyes, her heart so compassionate, having known such limitation and pain.

I can feel Lily's presence floating around me. My heart is beating furiously, as it has often done since Lily passed. I pull the blankets up even higher around my neck. I feel if I begin to cry, I will never stop. I muffle my sobs in the pillow.

"Why Did You Have to Go?"

It will be cold in the graveyard. I know I must choose just the right outfit to honor someone as special as Lily. I peer into the closet, and my eyes spot a long woolen skirt and cashmere sweater, a pair of fleece tights, an infinity scarf, and warm gloves. I will wear thick socks over the tights, my black Tadashi Shoji cape, and a purple hat.

I recall Lily's sweet and innocent face. Her rosy complexion, blue eyes, and gentle voice were pleading. "Will you deliver my service, Cynthia?"

"Lily, I'm honored. But don't you think others will expect a minister?" I wondered if her family would accept me in that role.

I remember her stressing adamantly, "Well, I don't need a minister!" After a moment of silence, Lily had collected her thoughts. "But I know you said in class once that the funeral is really for the living. So, I guess maybe I should have one. Oh, Cynthia, can you find a good minister? I mean a really cool one?"

At that moment, Lily looked so much younger than her years. She was trying to make sense of her short life, and her words were rushed in desperation. "Really, I want you to speak to them about life like you do when you teach—my life—because you know who I really am, and I know you can help them to know who I really was.

And you can help them to understand it all, I mean the world and all and why I had to leave so early, like you helped me to understand."

The eulogy I labored over lay on my dresser, my mind focusing no longer on clothes. I try to imagine delivering the eulogy in the graveyard. The only image that is clear is Lily's spirit hovering around me as I hold back my tears.

I swallow hard while my hands shake uncontrollably. Staring out the window, I spy a blue bird—the color of Lily's eyes—perched on the feeder, as if Lily is saying, "I haven't left. I'm right here."

A passage from a poem by the poet Rainer Maria Rilke comes to me:

> This is what the [bird] can teach us:
> to fall,
> patiently to trust our heaviness.
> Even a bird has to do that
> before he can fly.[2]

> *Oh, Lily, why did you have to go?*

> The bird took flight instantly,
> leaving the feeder and me ...
> empty.

[2] Rainer Maria Rilke, *Rilke's Book of Hours: Love Poems to God*, trans. Anita Barrows and Joanna Macy (New York: Riverhead Books, 1996, 2005), 171–173.

What a Gift This Lifetime Is

Just six weeks before, I am in the Detroit airport, and the concourse is buzzing. I am fortunate that we have not had snow yet. I now have a layover before flying on to Japan to work for three weeks.

I duck into a breakfast café and snuggle into a seat in the corner. Glancing at my phone, I am surprised to see a message so early from Lily. I'm wondering if she has received her diagnosis.

I hit direct dial, and Lily picks up on the first ring.

"Cynthia, I was hoping to catch you before you got on the plane." Her voice is slow and shallow. "I'm so exhausted," she whispers into the phone, as though uttering the very words might take her life. "I don't think I can do this again."

"Lily, are you okay? What's going on, honey? I'm here for you. We'll figure this out."

Lily shares the bad news. The breast cancer has metastasized. First episode of breast cancer at twenty-six, then again at thirty-three, and now at forty-two. "What can they really do for me?" she asks helplessly.

My heart is so heavy. I know there won't be much time left in the US to talk, and even though I can Skype from Japan, the time difference is thirteen hours. My night will be her day.

"I mean, Cynthia, I can't go through chemo and radiation. I can't be so sick again, and they're telling me I'm giving up if I don't." Her words are rushed and punctuated with short breaths.

"Cynthia?" Her voice trails off as if she's beginning to leave me. "I just can't do it again. I want to go home."

I pause for a moment, feeling my throat tightening. "It's your life, Lily. You must do what feels right for you. No one else can tell you that."

The truth is, how could I honestly know what it will be like? I do know she will be miserable. And Lily is so fragile.

"Do you mean that, Cynthia? I mean *really* mean it?"

"Yes, Lily. I really mean it."

"Cynthia, will you be there no matter what?" Lily says as if she already knows.

"Yes," I reassure her.

Then she hesitates. "But I mean will you be there *at the end*?"

I take a deep breath. "Yes."

"I love you, Cynthia." Lily's voice is stronger, and I can hear her relief.

"I love you, Lily. I'll help you in every way I can."

Lily's voice rushes in again, and I sense her relief becoming anxiety. "Cynthia, I need to understand the other side. I need you to go over again all that we talked about in our sessions and what we discussed in the class on the afterlife. Will you help me to remember?"

I sense her desperation, her need to be prepared for what might come. "Of course. Definitely. We'll go over everything. Don't worry. I'll be right there with you." Lily tells me she feels better knowing that I will be there. I promise to email her as soon as I arrive in Japan and that I will call her often. I remind her I will be back in three weeks and that we will do so much work together.

As we say goodbye, I can hear her choking back her fear.

"I'm with you, Lily," I whisper. A tear rolls down my cheek as I stumble, gathering up my carry-on to head to the gate.

$$\text{\Large ᨖ•ᨘ}$$

I arrive in Japan the next day. Fifteen long hours. The trip over the Pacific Ocean is always so humbling, with nowhere to touch down. I follow the flight tracker screen on the back of the seat in front of me. The tiny plane icon moves ever so slowly across the great abyss. Altitude, miles, speed, air temperature, and velocity are calculated. Here I am inside the tiny icon, trusting fate and destiny. A metaphor for life's journey.

What a gift in this lifetime that I can work in a different culture and connect with such compassionate people. I met my interpreter, Shiori-san, in the US. She was a university student who later became my interpreter for my work in Japan, and we stay with her family while we work here. When we met, we were immediately sisters of the heart. The synchronicities that caused our paths to cross were divinely planned; we have no doubt.

As the plane touches down, I am grateful for another safe landing. Shiori-san greets me at the airport with her usual big smile and large, dark eyes, her black, shiny hair pulled into a bun with bangs covering her forehead. Her Western attire today contrasts with what I saw years before when I first met her. She is relaxed and comfortable in her crisp white blouse and jeans. She hasn't abandoned her *geta*—her Japanese-style wooden sandals. As we leave for her home, we duck into the convenience store. I pick up a seaweed snack, java tea, and my favorite dark chocolate.

The two-hour ride by van to Nagoya will complete the almost twenty-four-hour travel. I breathe deeply, in and out of interrupted sleep, exhausted as the van jostles through heavy traffic. What would be my normal US day is now my Japanese night. Shiori-san and I discuss the itinerary, touching on details with excitement. I will see six clients a day for treatments, in addition to teaching two workshops. My typical three-week stay.

Finally, we arrive at the family home in Nagoya. Shiori-san's family is waiting for me, and we are so excited to see one another again. This is my tenth trip, and I am escorted into my very familiar room. Typical of Japanese homes, the rooms are small and compact by American standards. Real estate is at a premium, and every inch of space is optimized. My room is complete and efficient with a comfortable sofa bed, refrigerator, and hotpot. The floor is bamboo, the sliding doors are wood framed with translucent panels of rice paper, and the walls are decorated with murals of mountains with ghostlike trees against a pale blue sky.

My hosts have carefully placed my favorite snacks on a small table. They know my sleep will be interrupted sporadically with a need to eat at odd hours as I make the adjustment.

The most significant display in the room is the ancestral cabinet. The doors have been left open for the ancestors to greet me. It is a black-lacquered cabinet with brass handles that open doors to reveal gold icons of cranes, the symbol of longevity; incense burners, fragrances that have transported Japanese people to a different spiritual plane for centuries; and bells and Buddhas, all paying homage to ancestors who are captured in neatly arranged photos.

I love glancing at pictures of the Tsukamoto family carefully placed against the backdrop of purple silk. Always, the ancestors seem to know I'm here, as they show up in my dreams and sometimes as flashes of light in the room. Always welcoming and guiding. I see Grandfather in his uniform in World War II, wondering if he might have fought against my father. Life returns to center as his eyes meet mine in peace.

I plug my laptop in and send a short message to my American family—to my parents, to my brothers and sisters, and to my children who are now in their twenties: "Arrived in Nagoya—will be in touch through Facebook—easiest to use the FB messaging here. Much love to you all. Keep me in your prayers. You are in mine."

Then I email Lily to tell her I've arrived, that I miss her and love her, and that I'll call tomorrow.

Exhausted, I decide to dress for sleep. Shiori-san has laid traditional Japanese pajamas across the bed for me. The tunic top and long pants are silk and tied at the waist. White cranes fly on a royal-blue background, their golden beaks atop their long necks.

I put on the pajamas and stand in front of the dressing mirror to admire them. As I gaze at my reflection in the mirror, I also reflect on the life circumstances that brought me here from the other side of the world. This spiritual land embraced me, its people actively seeking intuitive understanding in relationship to spirit, eager to explore and understand the different dimensions of the universe.

My thoughts take me back to my early years. I recall when I was five, sleeping at home in my bed and being awakened in the middle of the night by a brilliant white light at the foot of my bed. At first, it frightened and comforted me at the same time. My heart beat fast as I pulled the covers up both to hide under them and to peer over them into the light. No matter how many times I opened and closed my eyes, the image remained. My heart pounded, but I did not scream. The light began to take on a shape. It reminded me of the angels on the cover of my prayer book, and even though I had never seen anything like it before in three-dimensional form, I knew that what was happening was special. Somehow I knew this being would not harm me. For the experience was more than just visual; it filled me with emotion. With love and with peace. It was a magnificent being. A divinity. This vision was the beginning of my experiences in seeing and feeling energy. Over time, this being became a welcomed friend.

At first I told no one, and I have often wondered why I chose not to reveal it, not even to my parents. I believe I was trying to protect the sacredness. I did not want anyone to dismiss or compromise my experience.

Yet, a year after the incident, I recall telling my grandmother. She was my confidante from a very young age. My mother's mother could see energy and never hesitated to speak about it in family circles. Our bond developed after I shared my first sighting. I stayed many nights alone with her in her two-story clapboard home on the hill overlooking the creek. Grandmother was no-nonsense in her approach to life. She saw energy, often describing her ancestors sitting in the parlor or walking about in the living room downstairs. I remember as a child feeling somewhat frightened at what she described, yet she reminded me not to be afraid of those who had passed; rather, she said, it was the living people who concerned her the most.

We sat together many evenings during my childhood in her overstuffed rocker, cuddled together as we listened to 78 rpm records and sang old wartime ballads with the vinyl record locked into a soft, scratching rhythm.

She always told me I was just a bit too skinny and she needed to fatten me up. She would bet me I could gain several pounds during the summer if she made us scrumptious breakfasts of egg, bacon, and toast with her watermelon rind preserves; lunches of fish, potatoes, kale, fried ham, and butter beans; and dinners of roast beef, mashed potatoes and gravy, collard greens, and, of course, cherry cobbler. I felt at peace in her presence, nurtured and fully protected.

I recall the day she passed years later. I was twenty-eight years old and was holding my first child, my eight-month-old son. I was living in the Midwest, far from home, and as soon as I received the news, my husband and I packed the car and drove with our son to the East Coast to attend her funeral. It wasn't until I arrived at the funeral home and saw her lying in the casket that I let myself cry uncontrollably, feeling suddenly alone and vulnerable in the world.

She was wearing her favorite dress—an accordion-pleated, lavender A-line dress with well-pressed sleeves, the one she had told my mother to bury her in. While I could not see her feet, I hoped she was wearing her shoes because she told me she intended to dance on the other side.

Now, here in Japan many years later, I look at myself in the mirror. At fifty-five, I am petite, not much taller than my grandmother's five-foot stature, and probably still skinny by her standards. My hazel eyes and blonde hair distinguish me among the Japanese, giving me an exotic look. Trying to fit in, I've gathered my shoulder-length blonde hair and twisted it into a bun, still attempting to master the art of using Asian hair sticks.

I reflect on the gifts Grandmother gave me. Would I be here in Japan, reading energy fields, teaching about other dimensions, were it not for my grandmother? She gave me permission to embrace my fears and to explore what I could become. Like Lily, I cherished the memories of my grandmother. When Lily would share stories with me of cooking with her grandmother or wearing her grandmother's pearls, I came alive with Lily in those memories.

In this dimly lit room far from home, I take a deep breath and feel myself beginning to trance into a dreamy state. The blue dome ceiling light is now casting soft shadows about the room. I slip back into bed, knowing rest will be important for the transition. Even though I fall back to sleep, I wake long before the sun comes up, the house completely still.

Finally, I quietly get up, tiptoeing in my room as I begin unpacking ever so quietly, hanging clothes in the closet, sorting out my belongings. I remind myself that all is well in my world and in Lily's. Our grandmothers will provide.

Hanging Lily's Heart on Hope

As a life coach and energy-healing practitioner, I had known Lily for nine years and had worked with her both individually and in personal-development classes that I taught. I had watched her transform from a woman who seemed at first childlike, isolated, and frightened to one who grew to share her deepest feelings with me and women in her classes, developing strong friendships. In fact, the support she received both in private sessions and in groups was paramount to her overcoming her fear of death.

Even though it was nine years earlier, I still remember the call I received from a business associate who would provide my introduction to Lily.

"She's a dear young woman, Cynthia. Been through breast cancer, and her first experience was at such a young age. She's now in her thirties and diagnosed again with cancer. I think you can really help her. She doesn't have much money, but if you could see her even a couple of times, I know it would be so healing for her."

So often I have thought about the importance of having strong boundaries, of saying no to requests that impose on my time and income. Nevertheless, to the dismay of some of my most caring friends, I continue to give my time and care to those with financial hardship. As I heard Lily's story, I knew my path and hers were destined to cross, and I did not hesitate to call her.

I remember our first session. I heard a soft knock, and I opened my office door to a young woman who looked apprehensive. I recall my friend telling me that Lily was in her thirties, yet this woman seemed much younger. Her blonde hair was long and straight, and her eyes blue. I could see suffering in those eyes, yet I did not evidence any frailty in her body. She was wearing an embroidered tunic over a denim skirt, and her shoes were espadrilles. What impressed me most about her appearance that day was the way in which she sheepishly presented me a bouquet of fresh daffodils, holding them up with both hands.

"Thank you so much. You must be Lily." I returned her smile. "How thoughtful of you. Please come in."

Her eyes were full of expectation ... desire ... innocence ... and pain. I asked her to take a seat on the couch and to get comfortable. As I put the daffodils in a vase, I offered her some hot tea. She readily accepted, seeming relieved.

"I'm so glad to meet you." I smiled.

"Thank you. You too."

I asked her what I ask everyone on the first day—what she wished to gain from coaching. "Well ..." She hesitated as her eyes wandered around my office. I could see her taking in the hearts, the framed prints, the Japanese décor. "I ... I want to heal myself, and ... I have breast cancer." She looked down and then said, as if it had just occurred to her, "I guess I just need hope."

As she looked up, our eyes met.

"Hope. That's a very good place to start," I said reassuringly. In my heart, I felt her uncertainty about life itself and about her own life. I wanted more than anything to inspire her, to help her understand, and to give her a reason to heal.

I asked Lily to tell me the highlights of her life story, as much as she could, so I could help her with where she was now. She proceeded to share that she was thirty-three and that there had been quite a few deaths in her family when she was young. People had died of varying diseases, but cancer was most prominent. Lily told me her father was in a nursing home, and she visited him daily. She was also very close to her mother. Lily was an unmarried woman with no children, and her family was dear to her. She mentioned spending lots of time at her mother's home.

She talked about her work as a landscaper. She had always loved plants and flowers, saw herself as an "outdoor type," and was drawn to all kinds of animals, domestic and wild. She loved visiting the zoo and spending time with the animals there. She said they touched her soul. However, now she reported feeling depressed. She was out of work, having breast cancer for the second time. The first time was seven years before when she was twenty-six.

The afternoon light flickered through the curtains, casting shadows as Lily wove her story.

"The first time, I was devastated. I felt a lump in my breast. I was so young, but, Cynthia, I just knew it wasn't good. And I was so afraid. I went through chemo and radiation, and so many of my friends didn't hang around. I mean we were young, and it was so scary." Lily twisted her hair with her hands, pulling it away from her face, and at the same time tensing her eyes as if she were trying to see things more clearly.

"You know. When you're in your twenties, you think you'll live forever, and then something horrible happens, and you realize that maybe you're not in charge of your fate. And you feel angry and sad and scared, but … you know you do want to live. And you cling to each moment, trying to hold on. Scared to feel."

I was overcome with reverence for this young woman who spoke so honestly of her fear and despair. More than anything, I wanted to reassure her and help her find meaning in what her life had become. I knew I could never really know how deeply afraid she had been or how much youth her illness had robbed her of, but I could listen to her intensely and honor her life story. I nodded for her to continue and asked her what she might need now.

Lily paused and then replied softly, "I just need hope. I mean hope so I can trust that it's going to be okay and everything is happening for a reason." Tears welled in her eyes as she continued, "It's such an awful thing and …"—she hesitated, trying to find the right words—"and I carry the heaviness all the time." Lily covered her eyes for a moment, then glanced around for a tissue. I moved the box on the table closer to her.

"And you look around at the world, and people are just getting in and out of their cars and going on with their lives … but your life has, like, stopped … and you're just wanting to do what they're doing too, just go back to having a normal life. You know, just like you had before." Her eyes blinked tears as she looked down at my coffee table where a small set of clay hands held a carnelian heart.

"I'm so sorry, Lily, for all that you have been through. I can only imagine how painful and difficult it has been." Lily held an innocence, a sense of youth and purity that seemed frozen in time. An inner light shone through her eyes as if the universe were mirrored in her. She held a specialness that touched my heart in a way unlike any other. I longed to support her, to lift her up after all she had been through.

And so I spent the first afternoon with Lily, hearing her story, helping her hang her heart on hope.

Before she left that day, I showed her a wooden box covered with painted hearts, opened it, and asked her to begin the tradition of pulling two Heartliving guidance cards[3] each individual visit. I told her that I created the cards to help guide people through their lives, especially their challenges.[4]

Lily's words that first day were Passage and Nurture:

"Passage: A rite of passage will lead you into new realms."

---

[3] Cynthia Bischoff, Heartliving Guidance Cards, Word-of-the-Day featured daily on https://www.facebook.com/Heartliving.

[4] I had created 108 cards to reflect what I felt were my heart teachings. Later, I found that there are 108 prayer beads on a string of mala beads. And in Japan where I work, I learned that there are 108 imprints on the feet of the Buddha, related to his soul's incarnations. Most interesting, in yogic tradition, I learned that if one can be so calm as to have only 108 breaths in a day, enlightenment will come.

"Nurture: Take good care of yourself, especially your heart."

We both agreed: how perfect.

I wanted to give her something from our time together that would allow her to continue her self-care. I reached up and took a Heartliving card set down from my product shelf. I handed Lily the set as a gift and told her to pull a word each day to help her focus her heart. I mentioned how powerful a daily ritual can be to help her remain hopeful. We set up our next appointment, and Lily promised to nurture her heart.

As I closed the office that day, I said a prayer, as I often do, for spiritual assistance, a prayer that I would be a container for Lily's healing, to help her see her own divinity, to help her have peace. While many clients have passed through my doors and taken residence in my heart, I knew that Lily would have a special place.

My Grandmother Gave
Me Permission to See
My Gift as Special

Early in my life, one very memorable experience provided me an understanding of the power of empathy. I was in fifth grade, and it seemed to be an ordinary day in our Catholic school classroom of twenty students. Each of us was sitting dutifully at our desks, practicing penmanship on our worksheets.

Sister Mary Thomas had just called Harriet, a frail girl, extremely quiet and shy with dark hair and large eyes, to the front of the room. Her plaid navy uniform that all fifth-grade girls were required to wear was wrinkled and dirty. Her face was smudged on her left cheek, and her hair was flat with her bangs stuck to her forehead.

I was sitting in the front desk in the middle row. I was given that seat perhaps due to my small stature and inability to see the blackboard over other classmates' heads. Sister Mary Thomas was a strict disciplinarian. She often made me nervous when she paced the room, although I was steadfast in my attempts to do no wrong in order to avoid her punishments.

As Harriet approached the front of the room, Sister Mary Thomas asked her to stand facing us. Sister stood on the side of the room out of our view and said to Harriet in the most horrid tone, "Harriet, look at you! You are dirty. A disgrace. Your mother is not so poor that she cannot afford a bar of soap."

Suddenly, I was frozen. I could not breathe. I stared at Harriet, and my heart was beating as though it would rush out of my chest. My face was flushed and hot. I had the most overwhelming feeling of wanting to save Harriet.

Harriet remained stoic, her face turning from pale white to bright red. She did not flinch. She looked out at the class, and I could see her lips quiver. Then I felt she looked directly at me, her eyes pleading. As tears welled in my eyes, I tried to blink them back, but they rolled down my cheeks. I wanted to comfort her, to run up and take her from this place. The only thing I knew to do was to pray that my friend, the being of white light, would help her.

Suddenly I noticed that white light was growing behind Harriet and around her. It seemed to be supporting her, enveloping her, and she began to shrink in proportion to it.

Sister Mary Thomas offered one last reprimand: "Tell your mother to wash you!" Then she ordered Harriet to return to her seat.

I watched Harriet's chest slump. As she passed my desk, she looked at me with tears in her eyes and a knowing that I will never forget. I knew that something in Harriet had touched me deeply and that I had extended my heart to her. This was one of my first experiences in which I realized that empathy could summon the being of light for comfort and protection.

For many years after my first intuitive experience, more and more often, I would envision the being of light that had come to me as a child. I began to find, inside the light, intuitions of the past and the future both for myself and for others. In fact, there came a point in time when I could call on the energy at will.

As a young child, I would wake in the early morning and glance at the wall near my bed. Shapes and images would appear in the morning light. I could visually draw pictures of animals on the wall at will—watching their shapes take form from broad strokes to fine lines and intricate details. I recall a specific recurring image that came to me, that of a lion. The lion was large with broad strokes and a finely drawn mane. Although massive and strong, I sensed the animal was gentle. I felt enormous comfort from this image. Much later in life, I learned what the lion stood for as a symbol: "Intuition is working. Now is time for strength of will, patience, and creative imagination. Do not force anything."[5]

I could see images and what I later referred to as "imprints" on flat surfaces—vinyl bookbags, floor tiles, wallpaper, bare walls. As I stared at the surface without trying to see—dropping into a bit of a trance state, imprints would begin to emerge as scattered lines that would come together to create pictures. I was intrigued by this ability, and growing up in a large family, I had enough socialization to realize that this phenomenon was unique.

I recall sitting with my grandmother in her parlor one evening. She was in her late seventies, and I was eight years old. It was summertime, and this room in the house was the coolest, always kept dark with the heavy drapes drawn. The furniture in the parlor was large and dark blue velvet, with pillows adorned with gold fringe and featuring the seal of the US Navy, souvenirs from my uncle who had served in the navy years before.

Grandmother was also decorated even though she was only sewing in the house that day. Nonetheless, she had on her red lipstick and white face powder, a necklace with large red beads, clip earrings to match, and her Avon[6] ring that housed a secret compartment that opened to expose a perfumed cream that Grandmother could conveniently access to apply on special occasions to her wrists and

---

[5] Ted Andrews, *Animal-Speak Pocket Guide* (Jackson, TN: Dragonhawk Publishing, 2009).
[6] "Avon Products," Wikipedia, accessed October 5, 2019, https://simple.wikipedia.org/wiki/Avon_Products.

behind her ears. Her hairdo was shoulder length and well arranged. She had recently visited the beauty parlor, where a dark rinse had been applied to cover the gray.

I was sitting opposite her with my new kit, working on a paint-by-number Jesus. We were chatting, and I began to tell her about my visions. She said she thought it was time for "our little party." We put down our work, and we went into the kitchen. She sat at the table, and I took my shoes off to stand in a chair to reach the top kitchen cupboard to retrieve the whiskey bottle and pour Grandmother her nightly shot. I wrestled some ice from the ice tray in the Frigidaire to fix myself a Coke in a special gold-rimmed iced-tea glass that Grandmother designated as mine. This was our nightly ritual when I visited: sitting together, enjoying our drinks, and talking heart-to-heart.

We talked about how I often saw images of animals, of people's faces, of numbers and letters. I told her how I could see them especially on flat surfaces, on walls and floors, and sometimes around people. She told me she could see them too. My grandmother gave me permission to see our unique ability as a special gift, not to be feared or taken lightly and not necessarily to be shared. This gave me the validation I needed.

Although I was confident, I was still very shy, yet I did not go unnoticed the way shy people often do. My shyness did not allow me to avoid the attention of bullies—a boy who would steal my lunch, girls who demanded I share my homework answers. Perhaps I was picked on because of my good grades that the nuns held up as an example. I was small and extremely sensitive. I made an easy target. Because of the bullying in school and the need to cooperate with my five siblings, I dared not be seen as different.

So the exercise of seeing energy was a pastime, entertainment, a secret friend during my formative years. This entertainment included imaginary trips to Jerusalem, to the birthplace of Christ, to the catacomb where Christ was buried. I remember beautiful images of Christ rising as the stone was rolled back, just as the nuns had shared in class. The images were my secret, but Christ I was allowed to embrace openly. I felt deeply that Christ knew me, and I knew Him.

As I grew older, I never rejected the image or teachings of Christ, yet my growing consciousness allowed me to take a journey into spirituality and world religions and to find unity in diversity. I recognized that all true teachings reflect the divine energy of unconditional love. Even though I loved my religion, by age thirteen, I was wearing a Jewish star, one I purchased with my own money earned from babysitting. I kept it inside my blouse in Catholic school. I had seen it in a jewelry shop and was so drawn to it.

So the nuns, the household, and my community had provided a focus of Catholicism, but as I grew older and my world and education grew, my spirituality became more universal.

My life has been lived in a highly symbolic way. Because of my early-childhood visions and intuitions, I have always been attentive to signs and symbols both in nature and in energy around me. I have discovered that imprints of information are constellated in physical matter, whether they be in people's auras or in the earth itself. All things are energy, and imprints abound. I often see images and symbols, faces, numbers, and letters in people, in objects, in the earth itself. I've learned that I don't have to know the exact meaning of an image, and if I need to understand something, I will usually be presented with the understanding. In fact, when I perform a reading for a client (look at the energy field around the person and take notes about what I see), I do not edit or judge anything. Frequently, what has no specific meaning for me has a clear meaning for the person I'm reading.

I recall reading for an elderly gentleman. I observed in his energy field an image of a blue horse. When I shared it with him, I did not know what a blue horse might mean. I was aware that the horse is a universal symbol for power, travel, and freedom. However, first I asked if a blue horse meant anything to him. A gentle wave of emotion seemed to come over him as he sank in his chair, closed his eyes, and tilted his head back. "It's my grandmother's horse," he said. "Money was tight when I was growing up, and my mother worked very hard to make ends meet. While Mom was at work, my grandmother would take care of me, and, boy, did I love her. I always took an afternoon nap on her bed. A blue ceramic horse was on her dresser, a prized possession, and I would gaze at it, sort of mesmerized while I was falling asleep. That's the blue horse you saw. Love and safety, that's what it means."

The transcendental image of the blue horse in his field was a sign that his grandmother's spirit continues to accompany him, watch over him, and protect him. This assurance became a new source of comfort and empowerment for him.

Early on in my life, the images that came to me appeared as static, and once formed, they did not continue shifting. For the past twenty years or so, the images are first static and now continue shifting, a phenomenon I have grown to refer to as "morphing," that is, the changing from one shape into another. It has become easier over my lifetime to receive intuitive phenomena, and I have been able to offer insight to those who are open and interested.

I have found that intuitive promptings involve experiences of sensitivity and empathy, healing, and visions. My work with Lily involved all these aspects of intuition. I was able to provide her with healing energy through time-honored methods I studied. I deeply felt sensitivity and empathy for her condition, which she told me was extremely comforting and healing for her. I also provided her with information that helped her to understand her world symbolically. I shared visions with her as they came to me: her grandmother's messages from the other side, frequent sightings of a seagull, whom she related to as her power animal representing freedom and solitude, and images of Archangel Gabriel, whom she said guided her.

Over the years, I have come to learn that unconditional love can create the healing white light and that it is this light that raises the vibration of cell tissue to a state of health. I also know that all of us can offer this loving, healing energy to others, as I did to Harriet many years ago.

When a Group Comes Together, It's Always a Destiny Gathering

As I continued working with Lily, I learned that she lived alone and had very few friends that she kept up with since her first bout with cancer. It was clear to me that she could benefit from belonging to a support group. By taking my signature program for women, "Leading from the Heart," she would become a member of a community of kindred spirits. I had taught consciousness-raising workshops for many years, and this program provided an initiation into this heart community.

Clients referred to themselves as heart sisters and heart brothers, and no matter the diverse backgrounds and preferences, we practiced nonjudgment as well as unconditional positive regard and support for one another. The goal of the heart community was to advance one another's understanding of life and to support one another through challenges as well as opportunities.

After several months of individual weekly sessions, I asked Lily to join her first Leading from the Heart group. "Lily, you mentioned the last time we met that you were feeling lonely. Would you be open to joining a group in which you could share your feelings with women who support one another?"

We were sitting in my office at the end of Lily's coaching session. She raised her eyebrows and, to my delight, responded yes without hesitation.

I knew that money might be an issue for her, and I wanted to allay any fears she might have about not being able to afford the program. I had an Angel Fund, I told her, to cover her registration. "Don't worry about the money. Others donate to allow someone in need to have the opportunity to take a class. Recipients remain confidential."

Lily told me she felt bad receiving the money: did someone else need it more?

"I would be honored if you would join us," I told her. "You are the perfect recipient, and after all, your card said to nurture your heart." Lily smiled. The heart groups had become a haven for many, and I hoped this would be the case for her as well.

I recall Lily's first evening in her group process. This evening was the beginning of my seminars in America for that year, and each year, I looked forward to the destiny gathering of ten women who would share their hearts intimately. Each woman would commit to the weekly group meeting, keep a journal of insights, and participate in the "heart box" project.

Twelve years had passed since I opened my office doors, and the space had become a center of positive energy, reflecting the sentiment of many who had come there to heal as they left gifts behind from their journeys. My office had been part of an old warehouse that the landlord had subdivided into units. On the walls and tables were many mementos: angel wings, hearts, mirrors, quotes, inspirational prints, a drum and rattle from South America, a Madonna and Child sculpture from Poland, origami cranes from Japan—a truly eclectic style.

The office "circle," as it came to be known, was organized in the first room as one entered the door. Our circle was created from chocolate-brown couches that sat opposite each other and were adorned with colorful pillows. On either side of each couch were overstuffed chairs in complementary colors. At the front of the circle near the door was a purple swivel chair that I reserved for my own seat to give easy access to the flip chart and books. Small wicker end tables held lamps and allowed space for teacups and personal items. In the center was a round coffee table with a white marble top and curved wrought iron legs. A candleholder of clay figures with arms joined encircled a large white candle that burned brightly in the center.

Everything was ready for our first evening, and all ten women had arrived. They ranged in age from twenty-five to sixty-six. Some seemed a little apprehensive, and others more self-assured, yet no matter her age, each woman seemed to have the same desire: to improve her life and to achieve greater balance. I noticed Lily's shyness at first was more marked, yet within a short time, she opened up and was laughing with several women she had met. "This is a destiny gathering," I told them. "I've heard that when a group comes together for a common purpose, it's always a destiny gathering."

Why did these ten women from different walks of life, different ages, nationalities, careers, needs, and backgrounds come together? Five hundred women had attended this program over the years. Each time, I knew that divine timing and order had brought that group together. I wondered how this group might be a destiny gathering for Lily.

Everything needed for each woman to grow would be found in the group and in the process, and commitment to attending and realizing that each of them was an important part of the process was stressed.

This first evening, each woman introduced herself and discussed her early family experience. All ten women told their stories briefly. When it was Lily's turn, she clasped her hands in her lap, and her shoulders were slightly bent as she glanced around the room, seeming hesitant at first. Then she caught my eye. I smiled at her, and she nodded and began. "I'm Lily. I was diagnosed with breast cancer, but I guess the most important thing for me right now is that I'm healing my body. Most days it's been hard to take a step when you don't know where your foot will fall." Lily pulled her hair back with her right hand, twisting it nervously.

"I've been working with Cynthia, and I'm glad I can be part of this group." As she looked out at the circle, she smiled, and I saw women smiling back at her. Lily continued, "I grew up in a pretty close-knit family. I was the youngest of three children, and I have an older sister and brother. My mother and father were good people, and my family has always been close." Lily spoke briefly about her special connection to her parents. She remarked that many of her days now were lonely and that she enjoyed the outdoors so tried to take walks at the beach, but often her energy was low, and when she stayed indoors alone, she got depressed. I was so proud of how much Lily was sharing and how honest she was being.

After each woman shared her story, together we examined beliefs that might be held to perpetuate ideas that might not be serving that person now. Had they held beliefs they now realized might not even be true? Were any old beliefs limiting their current lives?

I could sense that Lily was listening intently to each woman's story. Occasionally, she nodded at me, and I thought she might be reflecting on our discussion the day before. We had talked about ways in which she could release her fears and garner hope.

I reminded the group that the beliefs they held to be true became their belief system, and no matter how long they had held a belief, it could always be changed. Likewise, no matter how long they had done something or reacted in a certain way, they could challenge that in their lives now. We discussed the phrase "up until now" that I termed "the three magic words." I let them know that the "up until now" phrase could be applied at any time to remind them that they did not have to drag their history into the present. Their beliefs and their lives could change now to support their new understanding.

"Up until now." They nodded.

And so, in the evening light, the softly lit lamps cast shadows, and the candle glowed brightly as we sat in our circle. Some feet tucked up, some down, some hands folded neatly, some clasped as if to hold on, each woman shared her story as we maneuvered through the pain, the stillness, and even the laughter. "My mind is like a bad neighborhood. You don't want to go there alone," shared Susan, a compassionate woman who was never without her quick wit. Nervous laughter broke out, and we all nodded. Each of us knew that neighborhood.

As I explained the class project, I gave each woman a heart-shaped cardboard box and lid that she would decorate and share with the group. The outside of the box would be presented in the fourth session—designed to express how she believed she presented herself to the outside world. The inside of the box would be shared in the last session, and it would be designed to reflect what the woman typically held back, what might even be buried in her heart, knowing that if it were revealed, she might free herself.

With hope and intention, each woman signed a contract to agree to support herself and one another in the group process. I reminded them, "As each of you contributes and evolves, we all evolve." It warmed my heart to see Lily so eagerly signing her contract. She had participated so well in the group, making new friends, sharing her heart. Lily needed support and connection. I knew that no matter how many individual sessions I had with her, participating in a group process in a community of like-minded women and sharing her heart would be very healing for her.

"It's time to release your pain. Let today be your new beginning," I said to the group and continued with a quote by Anais Nin: "And the day came when the risk to remain tight in a bud was more painful than the risk it took to blossom."[7] Hopeful eyes met mine. Lily, especially, seemed hungry for a new way to navigate her world.

I addressed the group and knew these comments would be important for Lily. "While each of us may hold different beliefs about life, it is interesting to share our ideas and to learn from each other." I studied the group's reaction. Some seemed hopeful, some relaxed, and some pensive, perhaps not yet sure about opening to new

---

[7] "Anais Nin > Quotes > Quotable Quotes," Goodreads, accessed March 12, 2019, https://www.goodreads.com/quotes/876911-and-the-day-came-when-the-risk-to-remain-tight.

ideas. I continued to reassure them. "By listening openly, you can allow your mind to absorb new ideas while you remain completely free to accept whatever feels true to your heart. Awareness is really step one when it comes to life change. Every new idea you have opens a field of possibility for you."

I reflected on what Lily had said to me in her coaching session: "Cynthia, I've always admired people's openness to new ideas. I haven't had many experiences to investigate other cultures and beliefs, so I want to hear new concepts. I grew up in a family where we were told what to believe in. I've always felt safe in having beliefs that I thought were true, but now I feel open to expanding my mind."

In class, we talked about what we thought had been some of our most important life lessons. I asked them to consider what their life mission might be. I shared that each of our missions can be considered a noble quest that we fulfill as part of our spiritual journey, mentioning that many believe each one of us is born into our precise situation in life in order to fulfill this heroic mission.

Was there a certain theme that was playing out in their experiences? Several women commented. Raven, a grandmother in our group, decided that she had been integral in her grandchildren's lives, helping to raise them. Her theme, she decided, was family loyalty.

Asa, a graduate student from Taiwan, told the group that her name meant "born in the morning," yet she had also learned later in life, after meeting her Jewish boyfriend, that the name Asa was a biblical name that in Hebrew meant "healer." She believed that her mission centered around not only her own healing but also the healing work she was doing with others.

During the session, Lily was quiet but very attentive. Her eyes wandered around the room, and I could tell she was studying the other women while enjoying the stories each had shared about her mission. When it was Lily's turn, she surprised me with her confidence. Lily first turned to Asa and told Asa that her interest in helping others had inspired her, that she felt energized by Asa's certainty about her purpose. Then she said to me, "Cynthia, this is all so new to me. I know I have a mission, but would you just say a little more about how to figure it out? Maybe another idea or two?"

"Sure, Lily, of course." I leaned forward in my chair and clasped my hands under my chin, reflecting on how to proceed. "Well, you can think of your personal mission as being to complete a lesson in life and to participate in others' learning experiences. You see, everything that happens to you is important to your growth and life understanding as well as to others' transformation. We're here to help one another. Does that make sense?" Lily nodded, so I continued. "You see, your mission generally involves a special theme or overall lesson to work through in your lifetime. For example, some of you may have experienced abandonment early on, or you may have felt you had to be the caregiver of yourself and even your siblings. Some may have taken on the role of a rebel." I turned to Lily. "So, Lily, from that perspective, is there something you've had to overcome or work through in life so far? A specific primary lesson perhaps?"

The light had begun to change in the room as the evening sun was setting. Heart-shaped ornaments, crystals, and stained glass trinkets hung from a decorative horizontal vine that spanned the top of the large picture window behind the circle. The stained glass had begun to create a backdrop of color.

To be honest, I hadn't focused too closely on Lily that evening. I remember that first meeting I had with her and how eager she was to please, which conflicted with her need to be heard. So I listened attentively tonight when it was her turn. When she answered my question, she shared softly with the group, "You know, I think my illness has been a great challenge. I hadn't thought of it much before today, but I'm realizing something from our discussion. Instead of my life theme being about illness, I think it's about connection. I've felt disconnected for some time but realize my lesson is to stay hopeful and connected to people and to life itself. You know, I've been admiring the candleholder, those beautiful clay women arm in arm on our center coffee table. It reminds me of us."

What a dear soul Lily was. Several women told her they had noticed the candleholder too, and they asked me if I had intended it as a symbol of our group, of our heart circle.

I shared the story of how the candleholder had been given to me by a dear client, Marsha, who had been in many classes and had moved away after the sudden passing of her husband. The "circle of friends" candleholder, as she had called it, was just that—a circle of identical clay figures who were arm in arm, embracing the candle in the middle, the light at their center. Marsha's idea was that her place in our Heartliving circle would always exist whether she was near or far. Women might come and leave physically, she pointed out, but we were all part of a circle that could not be broken. Lily's comment that the candleholder felt like "us" let me know just how much she was embracing her new experience.

Lily took a deep breath and sighed. "It sounds like Marsha is a beautiful soul, and she's still here with us even if she can't be in the group as she was before. Her gift has blessed all of us."

I was so impressed that Lily had realized her need for connection, that she had discovered it as a theme related to her healing in this lifetime, that she didn't have to bear the challenge of her illness alone. She had made new friends and seemed to bask in the support they provided, and I could tell her anxiety had lessened and her heart was open.

As we began to bring our session to a close, as part of our class ritual, each woman pulled a Heartliving card from the box before leaving, shared it with the group, and recorded it. I wondered what Heartliving card Lily would pull in her first class session. I mentioned that each person's word was meant as a group word for all of us, while each woman's word was also specifically important for her especially. The class words were chosen:

"Determination: Set the conditions. You will succeed!"

"Thanksgiving: Something you've planted is coming to harvest. Results are forthcoming."

"Smile: Take a lighter approach to life. A smile reflects a heart at peace."

"Detox: It's time to unclutter your body, mind, and spirit."

"Manifest: You can manifest your heart's desire."

"Trust: Remain faithful to your ideal and find trust within yourself."

"Family: Have a closer look at your family situation."

"Receiving: It is important to ask for help."

"Approval: Give yourself your own approval."

And then I watched as Lily pulled her word: "Flow: Remove all resistances and move into a state of flow." Her eyes met mine, and we smiled at each other knowingly.

We closed with our first group meditation. I turned on soft music, and we held hands to create our first circle together. I wanted so much for Lily to feel the energy of the circle, of the healing light the circle produced for each woman.

"I will guide you through a brief meditation that I have set to music. It is designed for you to make a request and to manifest your heart's desire. Just allow yourself to relax and envision what you hear."

I began, "Everything in the universe is energy. You are energy. You are connected to everything, and everything is available to you. Take a deep breath and bring that awareness into your heart."

I could feel each heart beating.

"And now from the recesses of your heart, make a silent request for whatever you need."

Several deep breaths were audible.

"Envision and feel what you have requested."

I envisioned and felt them all healing, their loving hearts more peaceful.

"Finally, because you have complete faith and trust that you will receive exactly what you need on the journey, let go of any fear or worry, and as you do so, feel your hearts being lifted in gratitude … Thank you for being part of this destiny gathering and thank you for sharing your hearts." Holding hands, we smiled at one another while I leaned forward and softly blew out the candle.

Lily was next to me on my right. Hands were released, yet Lily still held on, leaned over, squeezed my hand again, and whispered, "Thank you, Cynthia. I'll see you on Friday for our appointment. I've had some important insights."

7

Up until Now

Lily knocked at the office door, and as I opened it, her blue eyes looked brighter than usual. She was wearing a turquoise sweater, and her blonde hair was pulled up with a clip.

"Cynthia, I loved our class! It made me think so much about things I honestly had never thought of." I loved Lily's enthusiasm and her childlike spirit. She seemed more animated than before, and I could feel a joyousness about her.

"That's wonderful, Lily. I can't wait to hear what came up for you."

I'd just put the teapot on, so I offered her some tea, and she accepted. We took our cups into the front room, setting them on the coffee table. I leaned back in my swivel chair, and Lily plopped onto the office sofa under the window. She took off her shoes to become more comfortable and pulled her feet up under her. She seemed more relaxed now.

"I hadn't realized before how many rules I've probably put on myself in my life. I love how the older women in class realized that they could still change their lives no matter how old they are or what's been going on."

"That's something I love too, Lily. The 'up until now' phrase can give us permission to change things at any time."

We heard a train whistle in the distance. My office was located a couple of blocks from a train crossing, and frequently the whistling train punctuated conversation. I always shared with each class that one of my very first clients was an elderly man who told me that he had grown up in a house close to the train tracks and that he loved to hear the train whistle, especially during the night. He said his mama had told him if something ever bothered him and he wanted to let go of it, he could just stick it on the train as it went by. After hearing that story, my clients came to appreciate the train whistle.

"I need that train!" Lily smiled, and we both laughed. "I keep telling myself that when I get thoughts like *I can't change things* or *I've never been able to do that*, I'll just remember your words 'up until now' and know that I can do it differently now!"

"Good job! I love how you're evaluating old stuff and letting go of what you no longer need." I took a sip of my tea. "Lily, what are some beliefs that you've placed on yourself that you could let go of now?"

Lily paused, seeming to avoid eye contact at first. "Well, I guess I never feel like I can make a difference with other people. I've always been shy, and mostly I'd rather just hang in the background. I've never been that sure of myself. So I really like being able to see things differently."

As Lily began talking about her feelings, I realized that she seemed clearer and more confident about who she was. "Cynthia, I feel like my cancer has been a challenge, but now I don't have to keep focusing on it all the time. Maybe I've been trying to run from it. I love in class when you said that everything you want is on the other side of fear. That is true for me, and I don't feel so afraid anymore."

Lily was moving through her fears and finding a way to transcend the limitations her illness had caused. In working with hundreds of clients over the years, I knew that when a person can reframe their circumstances and find meaning, creating peace is possible.

Lily shared with me that one of her earliest lessons involved needing to be sure everyone was okay. She said she knew she didn't need to do that anymore. When telling me this, she tilted her head to the side and looked directly at me, as though she needed my validation.

"Lily, that's an important insight. It sounds like you've tended to put your own needs second to everyone else's, and you know that now it's time for you."

Lily nodded her head and picked up a pillow, pulling it toward her chest as if to protect her heart. She hesitated at first, and her lips trembled. "The cancer, Cynthia, has been a terrible bully. The first time I was diagnosed and had chemo and radiation, I felt like I had no power at all. And I felt like other people my age didn't want to be around me. I was tired all the time and losing my hair."

I pictured Lily when she was ill the first time, clumps of hair missing and her scalp showing, her face pale. My heart felt so heavy. Even though I told her I was sorry and that it must have been hard, how could that ever be enough to say to someone in her circumstances?

"Cynthia, you know, even though I didn't think I'd die, I still had to create power in myself to fight back." Her voice became shaky as she recalled those days. "So, when you said in class that most challenges involve lessons about love and power, that feels right to me. I had to fight for myself and know that my life mattered."

"I admire you for how you have endured. You've gone through a lot for so long."

Lily shared that her feelings of power and optimism increased when her cancer was in remission, when her hair started growing back and she had more energy. Then the second time she was diagnosed, she told me she felt "beaten down" and that she was full of anxiety and could barely breathe.

The light coming through the curtains had dimmed as the clouds covered the sun, and the room was gradually getting darker. Rather than turn on another lamp, I knew that the dim lighting made the candle on the table burn even brighter, creating an intimacy that seemed comforting.

"And I kept thinking, *How am I supposed to beat it again?*" Lily looked down. "I had given so much effort and energy to it the first time. I thought it was gone. Then suddenly it was back. It was so unfair."

Lily paused, closing her eyes for a moment to reflect. "I just wanted to be like everyone else, just lead a regular life and not have to go back through it all again."

I listened intently, nodding reassuringly. Deep inside, I felt helpless. How could I possibly understand what Lily was going through? I was amazed at her strength. She continued sharing that she was always taught to do the right thing and that she realized that the right thing for her was to do what others told her to do. She mentioned that she wanted others to be happy. If they were happy, she could be happy.

"I guess the right thing for me was what I was told to do or what I thought would please others. What did you call that?" Lily's eyes were a little brighter, and she had adjusted her feet under her, now sitting cross-legged.

"I think you mean the idea that some of us seek approval outside ourselves?" I questioned. "We may not be sure we're okay or we're good enough unless someone tells us so."

"Exactly!" Lily affirmed. I could tell she was happy to find a language to make sense of her world. "And we let others tell us if we're okay or not, and I think we give away our power. I mean I know I did that."

I was so happy that Lily was finding a framework to help her make sense of her life. I realized how important it was for her to express herself and have someone validate her experience.

"Awareness is a wonderful step toward healing and reclaiming your power."

"Maybe that's why I had to have cancer twice. I had to do more work on my power, and I had to build my courage. It makes sense. It's really good to be in remission again."

"Absolutely, Lily. It is so, so good that you are in remission. Now you can continue to heal your body and release your fears just as you are doing."

"Cynthia, that quote in class really hit me too. It is harder to remain tight in a bud than it is to blossom! If my old understanding were written on a slate, I'd just wipe it off and write something new." I loved Lily's excitement and willingness to change. She was much less shy than before.

"That's beautiful. I'm so impressed that you are thinking new thoughts now." I smiled as I watched Lily put her pillow down. She picked up her cup and began twirling the tea bag around, bringing the cup to her lips and savoring the orange spices. "My health challenges have taught me a lot."

"They really have." I nodded.

"I feel like my issues have been much more than just in my body because I have to look at my spirit too." Lily was at a critical juncture in her healing process. She was balancing her fear with a newfound trust that she could understand it all. While I needed to be her cheerleader, I also knew she needed to feel her emotions deeply, reconcile her pain and suffering, and come into her own understanding.

As we continued the session, Lily said that more and more she was wanting to grow, that she looked forward to changing her mind and her life. She was working through her second health challenge well. She remarked that she loved having so many new ideas, and most of all, she felt that these ideas were going to change her life.

I was starting to see a woman who seemed much more sure of herself. A woman who was becoming alive in her expression and understanding and more able to be present in life without fear. Would Lily survive her physical illness? If she did not, would that mean in our worldview that her process had failed her?

I knew Lily's power would involve bringing her journey inward and that I would assist her in every way I could to remain hopeful and positive. I believe our life purpose is to discover ourselves along our journey—to learn who we are. I knew that Lily's evolving consciousness was key. Less fear and more love.

If Lily could make peace with her life circumstances, if her spirit should become victorious in the face of illness and even death, then I knew Lily would be successful in this lifetime.

My Developing Intuitive Ability

During summers while growing up in Maryland, I played outdoors in the yard with my siblings most of the day, riding bikes, making mud pies, playing tag or red rover, and often reading books in a hammock under an old oak tree. I always enjoyed the beaming sun and the homemade Popsicles my mother would give us as a snack in the afternoons.

Perhaps my favorite kindness bestowed in those summers was a special treat from my mother—an afternoon excursion to the local country grocery store, Frank's Superette. Mom would need a few items for dinner, and we were always in tow. She gave each of us a nickel, which allowed us to choose five penny candies, and oh, the choices! Candy lipsticks wrapped in foil, Smarties, Tootsie Rolls, root beer barrels, Sugar Babies, Dubble Bubble gum, and wax lips were among our favorites.

We could take our time looking at the items but could not touch anything until we were ready to request our five pieces. I remember the woman who worked behind the counter having lengthy conversations with my mother about children, school events, decor for the house, and church socials—and we waited until they were finished. Then Mrs. Lenny, her dark hair pulled tight in a ponytail and her white apron crisp, took our individual orders and placed our five candy pieces in separate very small brown paper bags for each of us, folded at the top, a personal treasure we coveted.

On a particular day when I was about ten years old, I had decided on my five pieces early and knew the conversation would continue for some time, so I began looking around the store and admiring the items on the shelves. I needed to stay in eyeshot of my mother, and I dared not disobey the rules. Yet the smell of cornmeal, cinnamon, fresh oranges and apples, even strips of beef jerky all filled my senses.

In the back of the store was a dairy cabinet. I walked back far enough to see the area while still seeing my mother in the other direction. I noticed a middle-aged woman at the cabinet with her back to me. She was reaching for a glass jug of milk. When she turned around, her eyes met mine, and I saw something I had never seen before. Around her were tiny images of a small child crying, a young woman scrubbing a floor, an image of herself at her present age looking so sad, holding the hand of a man, and an image of a much older version of herself sitting in a rocker, looking out a window. As I moved my eyes from left to right, I could see an arc of these images around the woman. At that time, I had no idea what they meant, but I felt in my heart a sense of longing and sadness in her. I accepted what I saw without fear or judgment and was grateful for Grandmother's guidance. Much later in life, I realized that these images were revealing time frames from her past, present, and future, which were contributing to the state of her current energy.

As years passed, I would come to validate these visions that I would see in the fields of individuals. While I could grasp images more or less at will, I didn't often "look" for them. To do so required a certain energy from me, and often my emotional state was affected by what I was seeing. It wasn't until I was introduced to various healing modalities and decided to be trained in energy healing[8]—breath work, Reiki (a Japanese stress-reduction technique), acupressure,

---

[8] Energy Healing, Science Direct, accessed October 5, 2019, https://www.sciencedirect.com/topics/medicine-and-dentistry/energy-healing.

and shamanic treatments—that I had a structure and a construct to perform what are called "readings."

Having read for many people over the past twenty-two years while offering healing treatments, I am always humbled at the intricacy involved in each person's field. Whether the person comes to me in a state of illness, confusion, anger, sadness, or in need of inspiration, I see patterns in what is happening in their lives. These patterns usually involve repeated opportunities for what each one may need to master, release, or heal.

For example, I recall a client who had suffered numerous abandonments. In our coaching session, we created a timeline of life events and found a repetition of abandonment that had continued to the present, from his father's leaving him at five, to his elementary school best friend choosing another classmate over him, to his first girlfriend cheating, and on and on. Whether a session is held in discussion of events or in an intuitive framework of me "reading" their field to help them, we piece together a healing method. What I help each person to realize is that it is not the repetition of events that provides healing, it is in responding differently to each new recurrence that allows one to heal all the way back to the deepest wound.

Often, in addition to images, I pick up someone who's passed on and wishes to make contact. For example, in reading for an elderly client, an image of a small child appeared, and later, the client verified that, yes, her two-year-old grandchild had passed unexpectedly several years before.

I remember reading for a person whose father had passed in a car accident. As we began her session, I picked her father up rather quickly, and he seemed eager to tell me that he was with Julius. The client sobbed when I shared this since her father had told her that he longed to meet his father in the afterlife. His father, Julius, had passed on when he was only nine years old.

I began in those days to believe in the afterlife, for I could see it.

Your Blood Follows Your Spirit

My travel to Japan had spanned twenty-four hours between flights and ground transportation, and no matter how many hours I am on a plane, I always find it hard to sleep both on the plane and once I've arrived. This morning, I glance around the room at the mural on the wall, the sliding door.

I hear a gentle knock and Shiori-san's voice. "Cynthia-san, so sorry to interrupt your sleep."

"Hi! Come on in." I spoke from the bed with as much energy as I could muster.

"I hope you slept well." Shiori-san has been up long before me, along with her sister and mother, always cooking and taking care of the details of our stay. She is already fully dressed in her coral tunic and white leggings, her hair pulled back.

"Yes, I slept pretty well," I reassure her. "Actually, very well for my first night."

"Could you be ready in an hour? We are to meet Tanaka-san at the coffeehouse for breakfast." I gave Tanaka-san a treatment during my previous visit. "He is now improving and wants to see you. He remembers your lecture on healing at the cultural center, and he has questions for you."

"Yes, of course," I reply positively, although my body feels stiff and my mind foggy. "I'll get in the shower now and start getting ready."

Shiori-san leaves the room. I get out of bed slowly and climb the narrow stairs up to the shower. The eight-year-old twins, daughters of Shiori-san's sister Shiho-san, shout as I pass. "Ohayou, Cynthia-san!"

"Ohayou, Aira-Chan! Ohayou, Seira-Chan!" I have known the girls since they were two years old, and they are now eight. They are usually dressed in matching clothes, often one in pink and the other in blue. They giggle at my attempt to say good morning while their two toy poodles yap at my feet in their own language.

I appreciate that Shiho-san has labeled all the bathroom products with English words. She loves order. My stay would not be as easy if not for her organizational skills. She often presents me each visit with new bath items to try—collagen for healthy skin, silk conditioners, washcloths made from bamboo. Her thoughtfulness is not unnoticed.

In Japan, I have found that presentation is so important. I truly appreciate the elegant simplicity. Decor in general is simple and natural, providing a type of clarity and beauty. I glance around this morning at the neatly organized bath items as I welcome the water, toasty warm, while attempting to wash away the jet lag, the stiff joints.

Once downstairs again, I check for messages. Nothing from Lily. I am worried. I have worked with her for nearly nine years and have developed such a loving and supportive relationship with her through coaching, energy treatments, and classes. I'm so grateful that she has found a community among friends she's met through her heart classes. Lily has been growing more and more aware over the years, living her life more fully and without fear. And now this third bout of cancer has me very worried. I want to protect her sensitive spirit.

I close my eyes while saying a prayer to bring Lily peace, love, and most important, healing. I dedicate the grace of my trip, the energy of this Japanese journey, to Lily. I pray that every breath I take sends her love. As I pause after prayer, I reflect on the world of chance encounters, how the hearts of so many have touched mine. I know that Lily's heart has touched mine in a way that very few have. I am grateful for our connection.

After making the bed, dressing comfortably, and packing my tote bag for the walk, I offer five yoga poses to my tired body before walking with Shiori-san to the coffeehouse.

The air is crisp as we step outside. The streets near the house are narrow with old-fashioned Japanese charm. Most vehicles are two-thirds the size of an American car or truck. I'm always amazed to see how carefully parked they are in the tightest spaces. Yards are small, almost postage-stamp size compared to Western yards, and each is adorned with interesting potted plants and flowers as well as solar lanterns, copper rain chains, Buddha statues, and bamboo chimes.

The most eye-catching home is on our walk to the coffeehouse. I look forward each year to seeing the ornamental cherry tree and blue hydrangeas in the front yard. The pink camellias with their lushly petaled blooms are also gorgeous. Near the road in small planters are also varied types of succulents. Perhaps what makes the home most delightful for me as I walk is how much I am reminded of my father's mother, my nana, who was such a gentle soul. She gave me my first hens-and-chicks succulents, and her yard had such lovely hydrangeas.

As we venture toward the main connecting road, we encounter markets, traditional shops, and Japanese-style inns. We pass the train station, a heart of activity, and see people of all ages walking quickly on their way to work. While the kimono is the traditional form of dress in Japan, few people wear it to work. Even though at first glance Japanese business attire seems the same as it does in Western countries, there are subtle differences that distinguish it. Most men's suits are black or navy with shirts and ties of a more neutral color. The key in Japan seems to be about blending in. Businesswomen also avoid busy patterns in blouses and choose more conservative dresses and suits as well. Shoes are clean and should be easy to take off. It is customary to remove shoes and leave them at the entrances to fine restaurants, homes, and many offices.

Young people with Western-style dress are among the group as well. Dressed in jeans and T-shirts, gym shoes as well as colorful sandals, they carry backpacks from which small chains on each zipper display the most popular Japanese anime[9] figures. An occasional kimono is seen should a woman or man be going to temple or traveling to a special location.

Past the train station, the streets are lined with traditional Japanese houses of dark wood alongside small shops, the doorways of many of which are decorated with colorful *noren*—cloth curtains that are usually rectangular and are designed with images to signify the product or service available behind them.

I seem to navigate not only by familiar intersections but also aromas; the rich smell of dark coffee, freshly baked pastries, grilled fish, and buttered croissants are favorites. The aroma of incense also permeates an occasional street, as many families light incense in the early morning in small shrines dedicated to departed loved ones.

I'm so glad to be here again, to have an opportunity to see my friends and touch new hearts.

Approaching the coffeehouse, I can see Tanaka-san glancing at us from the window, waiting patiently. His clothing is the traditional men's kimono. Once we are inside, he greets us with respectful eyes that glance down as he bows. His forehead is a map of wrinkles that speak of worries past and present. I know he is approaching his eighth decade. I have the utmost respect for him, and I bow with sincerity in return. Shiori-san translates his enthusiastic greeting to me. "Cynthia-san, thank you for coming to Japan. Thank you for helping my journey. Good to see you again. I appreciate you."

I thank him for his kind words. "Domo arigatou gozaimasu, Mr. Tanaka-san." (Thank you very much, Mr. Tanaka-san.) Even though I am aware that *san* in Japanese is the honorific term, I frequently

[9] "Which Anime Is Popular Right Now in Japan?" Mipon Anime Tourism, accessed October 5, 2019, https://mipon.org/anime-popular-right-now-japan/.

add the English honorific *Mr.* or *Mrs.* from habit, and I am so glad that my Japanese friends understand.

Tanaka-san waits until we are seated. He bows again and slides into the seat opposite us in the booth. His gray hair is brushed back, and his eyes are large, his jaw somewhat square. He has a kindness about him that eases my soul.

Shiori-san graciously asks for beautiful Japanese breakfasts and hot coffee. Soon, trays of *tamagoyaki* (egg omelet), *nori* (dried seasoned seaweed), and *okayu* (rice porridge) appear fragrantly before us with their welcomed aromas. The tamagoyaki omelet is rolled and fluffy, prepared in a rectangular pan, cut into square bites, and served with soy sauce. Sugoi! (Awesome!)

Tanaka-san smiles at me as I rave about the unique tastes of the Japanese food. While each serving is small by American standards, the blend of tastes is exquisite. Shiori-san tells me that Tanaka-san is so happy that I am here and that I enjoy his country, that he is proud.

I love how gracious Shiori-san is, how sweet and humble her personality. She sits erect, can handle any gathering, yet her eyes often well with tears as we discuss the plight of a client or friend. Several times she has patted Tanaka-san's hand and smiled at him.

Shiori-san tells me that he wishes to discuss life with me; then she clarifies, no, not just life but how he can heal his body through his spirit. She tells me that he understands that his cancer seems to be healing, but he says that he is not sure the way his spirit will go. Will he live or die? He says that he believes in a plan greater than he can control and knows that he must create wholeness in his body while believing the Japanese wisdom that "your blood follows your spirit."

She leans over to me and whispers, "Cynthia-san, he attended your body-mind-spirit healing lecture, but can you explain to him again how healing works and what he can do? He wonders if you must work on all three parts of yourself—body, mind, and spirit—not just the body when you are ill. Is that correct?"

Before answering, I pause, remembering a recent conversation I had with Lily in which she told me that until she had addressed her fears and found peace in her circumstances, and until she had nurtured her spirit and mind and accepted her body, she knew her healing would not be complete. I smile at Tanaka-san and realize how similar people of different cultures, faiths, and ethnic origins are to one another. Most of us grow up in one small corner of the world and are unaware of how similar we are to people thousands of miles away.

Knowing that I am simply a messenger, I proceed to explain to him as Shiori-san translates that I have been taught that the body is an out-picturing of the mind, an energy tool of the spirit. I continue that the mind is said, through its thoughts and beliefs, to impact the spirit and, in turn, the body. In this way, all three aspects of a person—spirit, mind (mental and emotional), and body—are integrated and create our health. Yes, the blood, or what we call the body and all aspects of matter, will follow or be impacted by the spirit, which is impacted by the mind. All aspects are interconnected.

Tanaka-san nods in agreement with my explanation and tells Shiori-san to let me know that he is working on his spirit. He knows that to treat the body separately, to focus only on the body in the healing process, would not be enough.

"Yes, blood follows spirit." The three of us nod in agreement.

I continue letting him know that, of course, his thoughts may from time to time reflect some fear and that this is normal. Yet when the fear arises, I tell him he can greet it by remembering always the larger perspective of his life, of his soul's journey. He can see himself on his life journey from a witness viewpoint, remembering that he has gone through many experiences, learned many lessons, and can and will handle whatever arises. In every moment, there has been divine order and timing to every breath.

Tanaka-san nods in understanding and says to tell me that from his Japanese upbringing he knows that for his spirit to be "correct," his mind must align with the highest spiritual ideals. He must surrender negative thinking, all concepts of separation, and raise his spirit through his mind to that which is positive and to that which joins his soul to everything.

I remember how important unity is to the healing process and appreciate my Japanese friends and colleagues and their dedication to unity in both their thinking and their healing. I let him know that he has a beautiful way of looking at alignment and health.

We weave our morning conversation in between bites of food and coffee, discussing the power of the mind and spirit in creating the body. We acknowledge that environmental and genetic factors can predispose a person to illness, and we also recognize that these factors may in some cases be beyond our control. Often, I reflect on Lily's plight, wondering the meaning behind her soul's choice to suffer so often as part of her journey.

Shiori-san translates Tanaka-san's concept that a person's overall health and challenging circumstances can also be impacted by a positive lifestyle and thinking, which together help contribute to spiritual well-being.

"Yes," I interject. "To think we can control life or our outcomes is not possible, but yes, we can contribute to positive outcomes. You are correct."

Tanaka-san nods and takes another sip of his coffee. He says he is willing to align his mind with higher thinking. He is not afraid to die, as he was last year. As he says this and Shiori-san translates, Tanaka-san surprises me with a smile. Something in him, he tells me, has surrendered, and he has decided that the Higher Power along with his own soul will choose for him the best decision, while he knows that he is responsible to contribute to his well-being every day no matter what. How similar, I think, to the surrendering that Lily has achieved on her journey. Her wisdom has come at half his age. How wise they both are.

I tell him how happy I am to hear his thoughts and the peace they have brought him.

Our waitress offers us more coffee, and we graciously accept. Tanaka-san then leans toward Shiori-san and tells her to ask me what might happen during death and in the afterlife. What is my American view?

I assure him that there are many views and ideas about the afterlife and that my own view is not so much American but has come from much reading, learning, and personal understanding in both my graduate studies as well as in my life experiences of seeing energy. My views have been influenced by a combination of religious, spiritual, and Western as well as Eastern principles.

Shiori-san looks at me, blushes, then smiles as she looks down and says softly, "Tanaka-san is sincerely wishing to hear ideas you have, no matter where they come from. He values your wisdom." I realize that I don't need to justify my thoughts, that my Japanese friends are simply open to spiritual concepts of all origins.

I thank Tanaka-san and begin to weave an understanding for my fellow journeyer. "In regard to death and the afterlife, it is my understanding that your spirit will be guided out of your body as you transition. In fact, some believe that a magnetic force helps your spirit release itself."

Tanaka-san nods with full attention as I continue, "In Western culture, many believe that you will experience a white light, like a tunnel that you will go through, while I understand that in Eastern beliefs, it is thought that you may cross a river. What is most important to my understanding," I tell him, "is that the life once lived here on earth releases as a new life comes forth."

Tanaka-san lowers his head in respect for these ideas. I can see that he is deep in reflection. I pause, and Tanaka-san nods for me to continue. "And yes, many believe that your ancestors will greet you with love to show you the way, and you may encounter angels and spirits who come around to help guide you into the next dimension."

Tanaka-san smiles, bows his head in agreement, then asks Shiori-san to translate a question. "I understand it is possible for spirits to attend their own funerals. I have always wondered if that is possible."

I return his smile. "Mr. Tanaka-san, I have heard that too. Yes, I have read and understood that spirits are often present at their own funerals. I believe they desire to reach out to comfort their loved ones."

Tanaka-san asks what exactly goes forward after death; is it our spirit? I tell him that I understand that we carry our mind-set of thoughts and beliefs with us into the afterlife. When we cross into other dimensions, while we release the physical body, we carry our consciousness. I understand that we have an overwhelming sense of being free and that we continue our learning.

Tanaka-san lets me know how hopeful he feels because he had worried that he might contribute to a wrong choice about life and death. When his wife passed away seven years earlier, he wondered many times what could have been done to save her. "If only" he told us he thought so many times. Now he says that he can relax with a greater understanding and peace, realizing that ancestors and helpers guided her and that her soul must have chosen the timing of her passing.

I reflect on a similar experience that Lily shared with me, marveling at the likeness of people's journeys. She told me that many people in her family of origin had passed when she was young, and she had decided that their deaths could not have been avoided in some way. As sad as she felt so often, she realized she had to honor her sadness but also accept that her ancestors were still in spirit around her. It was later in life she found peace in the idea that our souls are always learning through everything.

I share Lily's idea with Tanaka-san, mentioning how it comforted her, then add, "So, if you experience the loss of your wife as you have, and you are trying to understand the process of death and life, then your soul is learning."

Tanaka-san says these ideas are very comforting, and he shares with us that he understands that souls who have passed do not feel the physical separation like we do, and they can draw near to us if we need them. He has often felt his wife's presence. He asks what I think.

I nod yes, telling him I believe it is true.

"So, Cynthia-san, would you agree that we are not bothering them to call on them, we do not keep them from their spiritual work, and they willingly want to help us when we need them?"

"Yes, I would agree." I tell him they know we are affected by their passing, and they look for ways to comfort us. Tanaka-san seems so relieved. All of us, no matter the age, gender, or culture, simply need comfort and understanding in our life process.

In our corner of the coffee shop, we have huddled together and shared intimately as some people around us are holding loud conversations, while others sit quietly reading newspapers. I glance now to see Shiori-san look toward the door, making me aware that our time is up and we must go to another appointment.

We agree to meet again next time I'm in Japan and to continue our discussion. Although I believe Tanaka-san is correct in believing in a plan greater than he can control, I tell him how hopeful I am for his continued healing.

"Arigatou gozaimashita, Sensei! (Thank you, teacher!)" Tanaka-san says enthusiastically as he holds my hands and bows.

"Arigatou gozaimashita, Mr. Tanaka-san!" I return with a bow, knowing that we are all one another's teachers.

Shiori-san and I take different routes on the walk back since she will stop to pick up something from a neighbor while I will go back to the room to prepare for the rest of the day.

As I leave the coffeehouse, I thank Tanaka-san from my heart. I pray that, yes, his spirit will choose to continue living. He has no idea how much our connection and his journey have taught me. I am privileged to know his story and to share in his understanding.

Again, I reflect on Lily and both the smallness of the world and the similarity of our human journeys.

And So There Is the Important Connection of Hearts

In Shiori-san's neighborhood in Nagoya, the narrow streets are filled with quaint storefronts. I notice that an elderly gentleman and his lovely wife who own a bakery have washed the walk in the front of their shop, something they do every day to invite the customers. The smell of fresh bread fills the air. The wife waves to me through the window, remembering me from previous visits, and I wave back and smile as I pass.

Children of all ages are walking to school in their plaid uniforms and identical backpacks, referred to as *randoseru*.[10] Many people, especially the elderly, are publicly doing a traditional form of exercise in the schoolyards and near the temples, an exercise that allows them to stretch their bodies. I've learned it is called Rajio Taisou, which translates as "radio physical exercise." It was first introduced in Japan in 1928, and even today, many Japanese people still perform the exercise to maintain their health.[11]

---

[10] "Definitions, Randoseru," Stands4Network, accessed October 5, 2019, https://www.definitions.net/definition/randoseru.
[11] "Morning Exercise in Japan," Taiken Japan, accessed October 5, 2019, https://taiken.co/single/morning-exercise/.

I reflect on all the cultures of the world and how sometimes people can become so enmeshed in their own small lives that they believe that everyone feels, thinks, and acts as they do. Have I not done that myself?

I realize how much we can learn from one another. I am grateful I am exposed to different cultures and also able to engage in hearing about different lifestyles and stories. Lily told me many times how broadening her mind helped her to see her life in a larger way. If we leave with only our consciousness, I know how important it is for us to keep learning.

I reflect on the fact that so many people come and go in our lives, and I feel enormously grateful to have met so many interesting souls along the way. I realize how privileged I am that Tanaka-san's path and mine have crossed.

Like my chance encounter with Tanaka-san, many souls have come into my life that I will never forget. I smile to myself as I think that sometimes we need to take a spiritual pilgrimage, not necessarily to another country but even if only into our own backyard, in order to have moments of gratitude and reflection.

One person comes to mind who will remain in my heart forever, and as Lily told me, in her heart as well. On the walk back from the coffeehouse, I reflect on this chance encounter that changed both our lives, how a homeless man became so dear to Lily and me.

It was a chilly, winter Monday morning, and I had arrived early at the office. I cranked up the heat and made a cup of tea. As I sat down alone and glanced at my schedule, I heard a strong tap at the door. It was at least an hour before a client was expected, and I couldn't imagine who would be coming by.

I pulled the door curtain slightly to the side and saw a man standing at the door who appeared to be in his midseventies, shivering, wearing a pair of old trousers, a light windbreaker, and scuffed shoes, and carrying a tattered backpack. He had no coat, hat, or gloves on, and the temperature was below forty degrees.

"Yes?" I asked in a loud voice through the glass, realizing he could see me.

"Ma'am, could I wash your windows outside?" There is a large picture window on the front of my office and glass on the office door. I realized he was a peddler, maybe homeless, and looking to make a few bucks.

I cracked the door and said, "Yes, I think that would be okay. I need to see if I have any cash. How much do you charge?"

He gazed at the large window. "Six dollars for this size window."

"Okay, hold on. Let me see." I shut and locked the door and went over to my purse. I had ten dollars in cash. I figured he needed some warm food, and I was willing to take the chance whether or not the windows needed to be washed.

"Yes, sir. I have it."

The old man looked at me and said, "Do you have any Windex and some paper towels? I can do a real nice job."

You've got to be kidding me, I thought. *Well, all right.* "Yes, hold on a minute and let me get some." I closed the door again, went to the kitchen area, and retrieved the Windex and roll of paper towels under the sink.

"Here you go." I handed him the towels and Windex through the door.

"Thanks, ma'am. My name is Cardnell, but people call me Pop."

"Nice to meet you, Pop."

"What's your name? ... Are you the boss lady?"

I smiled to myself. "Yes, I'm Cynthia. I guess you could call me the boss lady. Pop, I need to make a call, but as soon as you're done, please knock, and I'll hand you the money."

"Yes, ma'am."

I sat back in the chair and could see through the sheers as Pop worked on cleaning the windows. I wondered who he was and knew he had to be cold. Although I could see him through the sheers, he focused on the window itself without noticing me in the room. He seemed intent on cleaning the window well and doing the best job he could. Finally, after about fifteen minutes, there was a tap at the door. I went to the door and smiled as I opened it. I stepped outside and looked at the window.

"You did a great job! Thank you, Pop. I have a ten-dollar bill here, and I hope that will get you some hot food. I bet you're cold."

"Yes, ma'am. I'm real cold. Thank you."

Then I hesitated. "Pop, you look like you need a heavier coat or some gloves." I looked down at the holes in his shoes and realized he had no socks.

"Yes, ma'am. I sure could use some. This is all I've got. But I don't have no money, so I've got to make do."

"Okay, let me see if I can help you." I hesitated. "Do you have a place to live?"

"No, ma'am. I don't. I used to, that is, before my mother died. But once't she done gave our house up—why, I was only thirteen—some man came to the house and had her sign off on a paper, and she didn't know what she was signing. I had to quit school and get a job, working here and there. Then my mama and my brothers and sister and I, well, we went from house to house. Now, mind you, I had a place to stay before Mama died, but after she died, it was no use. That's been over twenty years, and I've been making it as I could."

Pop nodded his head as he spoke, and I realized it helped him to tell his story. I could tell he was earnest. He wasn't drinking.

"Pop, are you able to stay in shelters? I mean it's really too cold to be outside."

"I do sometimes, if I can. But I tell you something. Sometimes there are people in those shelters that will take your stuff when you're sleeping. I don't have much, but I can't be having no young buck doing that to me."

I nodded my head affirmatively. "I'm sure that can happen, but you have to have a warm place. It's too cold to be outside."

"I know that's right." Pop paused and continued, "Boss Lady, I could really use a coat. You got some more jobs for me to do? If I could do some work for you, I could earn me some money."

"Well," I said, "I don't really have any work now that I can think of, but I want to help you get a coat."

"That would be mighty nice of you. And I need some gloves and a hat. You know one of them kind that brings the flaps down over your ears. That would be real nice. There's a secondhand store just down the street, not too far from here."

"Okay, Pop. Give me a minute and let me see if I have any money." I shut the door again and went over to my desk. I had forty dollars in my top drawer for emergencies. I reached for the money, closed my eyes, and thought of how much this could help him. *Would he buy the clothes?* I thought for a moment and then realized that I had no choice. I had to trust him. I couldn't turn him away. I wouldn't feel comfortable putting my own coat on to go home if I knew Pop was cold.

"Pop, okay. Look. I have forty dollars I want to give you." I could see the surprised look on his face. "I want you to be warm. I'm giving you this to go down to the thrift store and buy a coat, a hat, and some gloves. I'm counting on you to do the right thing to keep yourself warm. Can I count on you?"

"Yes, indeed, Boss Lady." He seemed to take delight in having a boss. "I will do that directly. Thank you."

"Good. You need to be warm, so I know this will help you." As he put the money in his pocket, I said goodbye and told him I hoped he would find some really warm clothes.

Pop walked away, and I reflected on how many different people there are in this world, all of us learning life lessons in different ways. I had no doubt that Pop's path and mine had crossed for an important reason that day.

My usual day progressed, and later in the afternoon, while I was coaching Lily, who sat on the couch near the window, I noticed through the curtains that a man was sitting right outside on the window ledge. *Oh, my God,* I thought at first. *I hope that's not Pop asking for more money.*

At the end of the session, I opened the door for Lily to leave. As we stepped outside, Pop got up from the window ledge. He was decked out in a long, heavy blue overcoat and had a red hunter's cap on his head, flaps down, gloves on his hands.

"Hey, Boss Lady. I've got something for you." Pop was beaming. He looked at Lily and apologized. "I know I'm not supposed to be interrupting with y'all having business going on."

Lily smiled and extended her hand to Pop. "It's okay," she said. "We just finished. I'm Lily."

"Yes, Miss Lily. Nice to meet you. I've got some business here with the Boss Lady."

Lily looked at me curiously, and I smiled. Then I turned to Pop and told him how glad I was that he found a warm coat and the perfect hat, just like he wanted.

"Yes, indeed!" He reached into his pocket and pulled out a piece of paper. He grinned as he handed it to me. "I've got the receipt for you!"

I was shocked. *He's giving me the receipt?* "Thank you so much! People don't usually come back and give you a receipt. I really appreciate that."

Pop told Lily that I had given him money to buy some clothes and that he had gone down to the thrift shop and found just the right things. Then he turned to me and said, "Well, Boss Lady, people don't give you that kind of money. You were good to me, and I'm gonna be good to you." He nodded. "And here's something I got for you. I think it'd look right nice if you're going somewheres special."

Pop had a friendly smile, large lips, and a broad, flat nose. His hands were bony, and his fingernails needed cutting. He reached in a paper sack and handed me a small bundle wrapped in tissue. I thanked him and opened it to reveal a bobby pin with diamonds across the top. He grinned and looked so proud.

"Aww ... thank you, Pop. That is so sweet. I love it. That was so kind of you to get that for me." The fact that I had paid for it didn't cross my mind.

Lily made a to-do over it, how beautiful it was and that she just might have to borrow it from me.

We all said our goodbyes, and that evening, I went home with a full heart. I was so grateful that Pop would be warm. Still, I couldn't get him off my mind.

The next week when Lily came for her session, she arrived early and asked me about the sweet old man and if he had come around again. I told her a little more about his story and how I had met him when he asked if he could wash my windows.

Lily looked at me suddenly with a huge smile. "Cynthia, what if we made Pop some business cards. Maybe he could wash other people's windows!" Lily was so excited with the prospect of putting Pop into business that I believe if she had the money, she would have bought him his own truck with his name on the side of it.

"What a great idea, Lily! We'll make Pop some cards and supply him with Windex and paper towels. He'll be in business!"

Lily and I met after work at her suggestion and began creating Pop's business card. We realized he had no address and no number but figured that didn't matter. His red, white, and blue business card read: "Handyman Pop. Please allow me to work for you! Reasonable rates. Great service. Honest. Dependable. Hardworking. Excellent with windows!" We printed one hundred cards and were excited.

Two days later, Pop was back on my ledge as I pulled up in the morning.

"Pop, you need some warm food?"

"Yes, ma'am."

"Okay, I have eight dollars I'm going to give you. You can go next door and get coffee and a sandwich. But listen, Pop, I have something to show you."

I gave Pop the business cards and supplies. I told him that Miss Lily and I were putting him in business. He beamed from ear to ear! And that was the beginning of Pop's business and Lily's and my friendship with him that lasted more than four years. Other clients became interested in Pop's story, wanting to know more about the old man who sat in front of my window from time to time. Most of them allowed Pop to wash their car windows, no matter the season.

After getting some history from him as our relationship progressed, Lily and I realized that he had been a painter for part of his life and would be eligible for social security. I was able to find a caseworker who could help him. Pop was so pleased to find out that he could receive $400 a month.

I put out an email to clients with Pop's story, and several clients helped me find him a cheap efficiency apartment. Lily managed the donations. People gave her items for his new place—a microwave, linens, towels, dishes. Pop told me he thought he was rich! My daughter was twelve years old at the time, and she and I went shopping and bought Pop a warm blanket, pillow, food, and, through her persuasion, a teddy bear. "Mom," she said, "he has to have one!"

"Of course he does! Of course."

And so there is the important connection of hearts. If one heart reaches out, another one does too, and so with our hearts connected, we help one another.

My favorite outcome of Pop coming into my life is that he seemed to create a project of love and compassion for Lily. She especially wanted to save Pop from suffering. Often she would show up early for an appointment or stay after so she would have time to chat with Pop. When he needed personal items, I could count on Lily to help him. She took many trips to the Dollar Tree store to buy him basic supplies. I remember one day she choked up as she told me that she and Pop had gone to lunch together and he told her how much he missed his mother. She missed her mother too, she told me.

Other clients, especially a dear woman named Faye, whom Lily had befriended in the classes, took a special interest in Pop, making sure that he had extra clothes or items as he needed them. With their help, I could count on Lily and Faye to be sure Pop was okay.

I remember the first holiday after I met Pop, I went to Indiana to visit relatives. I thought of my clients, pleased to know that Lily was staying with her family and that her cancer was in remission. As I weaved through the farms on the long drive and saw occasional snow, I reflected on whether Pop was okay. Was he warm enough? I couldn't get him off my mind.

When holiday presents were exchanged, I was given a picture that had been in the family and packed away for years—an antique picture of a cardinal perched on a branch that my sister-in-law had resurrected from her mother's basement, that she said for some reason made her think of me. I was shocked when I opened it, for no one knew Pop's name was Cardnell, or "Cardinal," as he pronounced it.

Although I was unaware at first how profound the relationship with Pop would become for me, I was most grateful that the relationship that Lily created with Pop was truly transformative for her. She commented about him often, looking after him, often sitting at a picnic table near my office to share snacks with him and to hear his stories.

During one coaching session, Lily shared that her relationship with Pop made her aware that people everywhere are struggling and that some, like Pop, had only a fraction of the resources she had. Often they were trying to make ends meet with little support from others. She said she remembered at her church while growing up seeing cropped pictures of starving children from other countries. Her family contributed in ways to help them, but Lily said she always wanted to hold these children and love them. I thought of my own experience with Harriet in fifth grade. It was her experience with Pop, Lily told me, that made her both grateful and humble, compassionate and aware of what each of us could do for one another. She said that as different as we think we are from others, we are much more similar than different. Each person, she told me, was divine.

I had previously taught literature classes at a university, and a quote from an essay by Ralph Waldo Emerson, American philosopher, immediately came to me. I shared it with Lily: "The progress of the intellect … neglects surface differences. To the poet, to the philosopher, to the saint, all things are friendly and sacred, all events profitable, all days holy, all men divine."[12]

---

[12] "Ralph Waldo Emerson," Wikiquote, accessed June 19, 2019, https://en.wikiquote.org/wiki/Ralph_Waldo_Emerson.

A Dress Rehearsal

The first day in Japan was a full workday, and I was feeling the jet lag. That night in my Japanese room, I lay in bed thinking again about Tanaka-san and our conversation and how blessed I was to know him. His heartfelt questions touched my soul. How many people might enrich and expand their lives if only they were open to one another?

My mind wandered again to Pop and how in the short amount of time I had known him, we had been each other's teachers. So many times Lily had asked about Pop or let me know she had seen him in the streets in town, handing out his cards proudly. I knew how much he had touched her heart.

I remember Lily telling me once, her eyes full of spirit and her face glowing, "You know, Cynthia, Pop is definitely in our soul group!" to which I replied, "I have no doubt."

Lily had such compassion for anyone who was suffering for whatever reason. Perhaps her own suffering had opened her heart to others' pain. Lily thought it was especially important that Pop not feel alone. In fact, when Pop was dying, we took turns visiting him in the hospital and the nursing home every day. We phoned each other in the evenings to fill the other in on how he was doing.

"You know," Lily told me, "I don't want Pop to be alone, but I also don't want him to be afraid, especially about dying." Then she continued, "Cynthia, I've talked to him and told him a few things we've been going over in our class about the afterlife, like, you know, the stuff about reincarnation being a possibility. He said it sure would be good if he could come back again and know us!" I remember we both laughed, and then Lily continued, "I hope he has more power next time without the struggles. He has such a good heart. You know, the basic things we take for granted mean so much to him."

I thought for a moment about Pop and Lily and how each had come into my life at different times for different reasons and how the circle of life brought us together, as often happens in mysterious ways. Yes, we are one another's teachers.

Suddenly, my phone screen is animated in the dark. I look down and see a call from Lily.

"Lily, hello!"

"Cynthia? It's so good to hear your voice." Lily spoke in a hushed tone.

"You too. How are you?"

"The doctors told me that the cancer is in my bones." Her voice trails off.

I find myself barely breathing.

She continues, "They are not hopeful and just want me to be comfortable. Cynthia, I need to remember what you've taught me in classes. You know, what we can expect on the other side. I'm scared." I am not prepared to lose Lily, not prepared for her to suffer, nor for her to be so afraid. I am in shock.

"Lily, I'm so sorry. I'll help you. I'll be home in no time. I will help you with everything." The words rush from my lips. I feel overwhelmed. I want to be with Lily at this moment, and I am thousands of miles away. I reassure her that we can talk each day, and any time she needs to, she can call. Even during my night in Japan, I tell her, if she gets afraid, she can call. I'm right here.

As we say goodbye, I let Lily know that I love her. There is a brief silence, and then Lily replies in a trembling voice, "I love you too."

I lie in bed barely breathing. I am so worried. I can't wait to get back home. I feel an urgency to protect her from her fears. To be there for her, exactly as she needs me. I can't bear that she might feel alone and isolated. My heart is hammering inside my chest. I curl up tight in my bed. I bury my face in my hands. My tears flow freely as I gasp for breath.

I call on Pop to help from the other side. I beg him. "Pop, please help Lily as Lily helped you."

I am riddled with worry. I will help her through whatever lies ahead. I cry myself to sleep.

$$\langle \cdot \rangle$$

In the middle of the night, my mind rambles, and I remember the shock Lily and I went through when, shortly after Pop got his apartment, two young boys came in during the night and beat him up. Pop showed up at my office the next day with his ribs bandaged, having found his way into the street that night, where someone had picked him up and taken him to the hospital emergency room. He told Lily and me later he thought the boys were just angry at him that somebody had helped him and jealous that he had found a place to stay. Two of my male clients who had assisted Pop in moving in confirmed the damage to his property, but before they could help him make his apartment secure, Pop had decided it wasn't safe to stay there any longer. I remember we felt so defeated when Pop was homeless again. Lily couldn't stop crying. Her dear friend was alone and afraid.

Shortly after, Pop was on the street again. I received a call at my office, and as soon as it said, "This is the jail. You have a call from Pop," while I had been told not to accept any calls from jail, this one I knew I needed to take.

It turned out that Pop had been found in an old abandoned house and picked up for parole violation. He asked me to come to help him.

Lily had stopped by my office at the end of the day. I told her the situation and that I would try to visit Pop at the jail to figure out what was going on. "Cynthia," she said, "we have to help him. If you go see him, I want to go with you."

That was the first of many times Lily and I visited Pop in jail over the next year. Lily and I also composed letters together that we sent him, and she especially loved writing to him about the birds at her feeder and one cardinal that kept coming that she had named "Pop."

I will never forget our first visit to the jail. Lily met me at the office. Neither of us had ever visited a jail, so we had no idea what to expect. We ended up having to park quite far from the building. As we walked down the street, we noticed a blue bird on a branch squawking at us. As we came closer, the bird jumped out of the tree and literally onto the concrete sidewalk in front of us. We laughed and decided that it was a mama bird whose babies were not going to be harmed. Lily remarked, "Maybe it's Pop's mother who's come back to tell us to take care of him." We both laughed.

Once in the cinderblock building, we had to report to the officer and put our purses in a locker. We were not allowed to bring anything into the visitation area, including pen, paper, phone, and so on. After a grueling two-hour wait of sitting on the cold floor, we were finally called to go up the elevator to the visitation area.

As we stepped off the elevator, we both turned to see Pop sitting in a window behind glass and bars. His face broke out into an enormous grin. With one of his front teeth missing, he looked like an old man and a child too. Through the hole in the glass, he exclaimed, "Boss Lady! Lily! What y'all doing here?"

"Pop, what are *you* doing here?" Lily asked, and we all laughed. Lily was so relieved to see Pop. She squinted her eyes when she smiled.

"Well," he continued, "I didn't know it would be you two. They told me two people were here to see me, and I asked who it was, and they told me two street people!" We laughed again, and I was so glad to see Pop's smile and to hear his voice.

Pop was wearing a wristband that had eight numbers on it. I asked Lily to memorize the first four and I would memorize the last four. My idea was that with the numbers, we could try to find out why he was in jail.

When I asked him what happened, he said, "Well, you know when you all helped me get that place, well, I had a parole officer before that. I used to sleep in empty houses. After I changed my life, I forgot I had that old life. Then those boys beat me up, and I had to find old places to stay again. This time when the cops found me, they could tell I had a record for doing that before, and I had to come back in." Pop weaved his story as he shook his head from side to side, occasionally showing his toothless grin.

"You know, they got a canteen here where you can get you a Coke and some chocolate and stamps and a card you can send to somebody. I really need me some money for my canteen. That way I can send you cards now and then. I need to keep you knowing about what's happening here." Pop had no family. Lily, several clients, and I had adopted him.

I sent money for Pop's canteen account, and Lily gave Pop her address so that he could send cards to us. Besides visiting him and sending him cards, Lily took such delight in bringing cards she had received from Pop to my office. He was quite an artist and used to love to send drawings. Lily was so proud of him that she told me she put one of his drawings on her refrigerator. I know helping Pop was a true joy for her, as it was for me. Lily loved a sculpture that Pop had made for me while in jail. He told me it was that of "a man looking up to God." In some ways, Lily and Pop were kindred spirits, both fragile yet strong.

A year passed, and after Pop was released from jail, he came back into our lives. Before long, Lily said to me, "Cynthia, I think

Pop has something wrong with his neck. Did you notice the lump on the right side of his neck?"

I had noticed it a few days before, and through our insistence to be checked and Lily's effort, Pop allowed us to drive him to the hospital.

When Lily, Pop, and I arrived at the emergency room, Pop was checked in. I was unaware at the time that he had listed Lily and me as next of kin. He insisted on our being with him when he saw the doctor. After an hour or so in the waiting area watching cartoons, which Pop seemed to enjoy, the three of us were escorted to the cubicle where he would be seen.

A young male doctor walked in and hesitated when he saw Pop on the bed, Lily sitting in a chair, and me standing. I appreciated that he directed his attention toward Pop and allowed Pop to answer his own questions.

Several tests were done, and the doctor returned to the room. The doctor told him in as kind a way as possible that he had an advanced stage of throat cancer and needed to be admitted.

I remember the shocked look on Pop's face. His response to the doctor surprised me. He told the doctor that he still had a lot of work to do, that he had just gotten some new jobs and that he had to keep his commitments, that he couldn't stay in the hospital very long.

Lily looked at me with tears brimming in her eyes, her lips trembling. She turned her head away from Pop. I was unable to move or speak, knowing that I had to hold all of us together. I took a deep breath and leaned over to Pop and reassured him that he had a wonderful doctor who would help him and that we would be there with him. As I hugged him, Pop's eyes filled with tears. We all cried that day.

Pop was hospitalized, and after three weeks, as death became imminent, he was transported to a nursing home. Lily, Faye, and I took turns visiting him daily until he died. We shared our special moments with Pop with one another, describing his antics: the time he tried to bribe the orderly to help him break out of there, the day he insisted that Faye bring him a pair of shoes because someone had stolen his, and the time he tried to call out on the hospital phone for baby-back ribs. Lily made him homemade thinking-of-you cards and took him balloons and flowers and sat in his room watching cartoons with him often, all so that, as she put it, "he would just know someone was there for him."

Lily shared with me several days before Pop passed that she had come to see in Pop her own vulnerability, her own need for love and connection. She knew that, as she put it, our souls were meant to connect with certain people in our lifetimes. She felt that Pop was her earthly brother.

After his death, we had no idea where Pop's body was taken. Lily researched and found that homeless people are buried by the city in a special area of the graveyard that remains unnamed, and the city does not reveal the information to the public. I could feel her disappointment as she shared, "All I wanted to do was put flowers on his grave to honor him."

Pop's passing affected Lily deeply. She spoke of him often in both individual sessions with me and in classes. She would reflect on his life often and share her thoughts about how difficult Pop's life had been, questioning why some people must go through so much. I knew she needed a ceremony for Pop to allow him to be honored.

I told Lily, "Let's have our own celebration of Pop's life. We'll invite anyone who wants to pay tribute to Pop to come to my office."

Nothing could have made Lily happier, so she orchestrated the event. She had an idea for us to have votive candles in a bowl on the center coffee table where we would each light one in honor of Pop. A group of more than twenty people gathered (those of my clients who had come to know him as they came for appointments and saw him sitting on my window ledge so often), and we all shared stories about him, laughing and crying, sometimes at the same time. Each of us lit a candle in his honor.

As we ended our gathering, Lily surprised us all by giving each of us a small cardinal cut from construction paper. She had drawn and cut each one perfectly. She thought it would be wonderful if we would close our tribute by holding a cardinal and singing together the song "You Raise Me Up!"[13] She had found the words on the internet and copied them for us to sing together. She had also brought the CD to play while we sang. She knew that Pop had raised us up as we had helped him. At the time, were we unaware that Pop's ceremony might be a dress rehearsal for what would come to pass for Lily?

I plead now with Pop, "Please help Lily, so young, so loving, so innocent. Please raise her up."

---

[13] Josh Groban, "You Raise Me Up!" YouTube, accessed March 15, 2019, https://www.youtube.com/watch?v=aJxrX42WcjQ.

12

"I Wish I May, I Wish I Might, Have This Wish I Wish Tonight."

It was the last session of my eight-week program, Leading from the Heart, the last day of the first program that Lily had attended, and each woman was to share the inside of her heart box this evening. This was the first of many of my eight-week programs that Lily would participate in over a nine-year connection. Yet I knew this first heart experience would be so powerful for her.

To decorate the inside of the box, I asked the women to reflect: What did you usually hide from others, or what was deeply special to you? Being vulnerable would require courage and would be honored and appreciated by each of us. There would be no judgment.

When it was her turn, Lily removed her heart box from a velvet bag. She had shared the outside of the box in an earlier session; her box was painted green for the gardening she loved, with images of cats and dogs—her favorite "people," as she told us. She had glued tiny shells around the outside edges for her love of the ocean and painted a seagull in the middle of a blue sky. She told us she considered the seashore a very healing place and the seagull perhaps her favorite animal. It often flew alone, as she told us she did, and she loved to watch it soar.

"It was not easy for me to decorate the inside of the box," she told the group, clutching the box close to her heart. "You know, the part Cynthia asked us to consider: *what do I hold back?* Well, I thought about that so much." She paused, looked down, and twisted her hair back away from her face. "I have fears that I try to hide, and I know they are in my heart, not always known to anybody else, so I gave a lot of thought to how I could decorate what the inside of my heart is like: *how can I represent it all in my heart box?*"

Several women nodded in agreement at how hard decorating the inside of the box had been for them too. Lily seemed relieved and continued. "Then there is also the love of my family I want to express, especially the closeness I always held with them. So my box has good stuff and fears combined." Lily's voice shook, and then a tear slid down her cheek. Soon more fell in an unbroken stream. Marva, a kind woman sitting next to Lily, reached for the tissue box, handed Lily a tissue, and took one for herself. Soon the tissue box was passed around the room.

Lily looked up at the group again. "There were deaths in my family when I was young, and my grandmother helped me feel safe and protected. I remember her sweetness and how she loved to cook and how she let me help her even as a little girl. I needed to put her energy in the box."

As she spoke, Lily gently lifted the lid of her heart box. I watched as the women looked on. She had painted the inside of her heart deep purple, which she told us was her favorite color, mentioning that for her, purple balanced the liveliness of red with the calming quality of blue. It gave her a feeling of mystery, and there was so much she told us that her heart did not yet understand, so much about the world, about life and death, that she didn't know.

Lily had painted small glittery stars under the lid of her heart against the dark purple sky. The stars, she mentioned, were to remind her of a poem her mother had taught her, which she used to say as a child as she gazed out her window into the night sky: "Star light, star bright, first star I see tonight. I wish I may, I wish I might, have this wish I wish tonight."[14]

So many times over so many years, she had made wishes, she said, as we all do. And her wishes had changed many times. Now, she told us, she wished for life, to live longer. She had met a man, and she enjoyed his company. He didn't seem afraid of her breast cancer diagnosis. Maybe, she said, he had made peace with life. He didn't seem afraid to be with her as she was. We all sighed, feeling her sense of peace.

I was aware of Lily's innocence, of a kind of timeless purity that she possessed. It was as though a part of her had stopped growing at a young age, perhaps due to her illness. I felt that sharing her heart box with us made her vulnerable in a way that could provide her a connection to healing her own inner child. In some ways, Lily was childlike, and in other ways, wise beyond her years.

Lily reached into the box and removed a beautiful pearl necklace, telling us that it had belonged to her grandmother. She had placed it in her heart for two reasons: First, it was to represent her grandmother's love and all the love she had received in her lifetime that she told us she held in her heart. Second, she said the necklace reflected what I had shared in my teaching about the pearl necklace as a symbol. She said this teaching was very meaningful for her.

Lily was referring to the symbolism of the pearl necklace that I had learned about in metaphysics classes. In some cultures, the pearl necklace was said to represent the soul's evolution. Each pearl stood for a different lifetime in a string of lifetimes, and each pearl was an opportunity for us to learn something important about the human condition. And so Lily told us that she understood from what I had shared that we have many lifetimes to learn the human condition as we deal with different circumstances and life lessons.

How well she had understood and how much it seemed to calm her, I thought.

---

[14] "Star Light, Star Bright," Poetry Foundation, accessed March 17, 2019, https://www.poetryfoundation.org/poems/46976/star-light-star-bright.

"And my fears?" Lily said, reaching into the box underneath the necklace and taking out tiny glass teardrops that glittered not unlike the stars. "I put these glass drops in my heart to represent tears. I can be hopeful one moment and then frightened the next. But learning what Cynthia told us, to be the witness to a bigger picture of life, I know I am larger than any moment of fear."

Lily was hungry for ways to understand her life, her challenges, and her journey. I had no doubt she was exploring new territory and finding solace in new ideas.

To follow the Heartliving tradition, Lily passed her heart around the circle, each woman holding it and commenting on its beauty, and finally the heart returned to Lily, who placed it on the coffee table, leaving it open as was our tradition. Then the next woman and the next shared until ten opened hearts circled the candle, all different and unique, as was each woman's story, all honored and open.

In closing our program, I reminded the group of a few Heartliving principles. "As we go through the journey, we maneuver through challenges, which are really just opportunities for what we need to master, let go of, or heal. Having a different response this time than we may have had before is what heals us."

I glanced at Lily and thought of her past as I shared, "As children, we had very little power when we were wounded by a person or an event. As adults, we have the power of choice in how to respond to everything."

Giulia, an insightful, fun-loving young woman from Italy, spoke up. "Cynthia, have you ever thought that you can create your own life review in the middle of your life? I mean review every big thing that's happened and then decide to change some stuff up? You know, before your life is over?"

"Absolutely, Giulia. You can bring new awareness into your story, and you can change anything you wish by changing your thinking."

I reminded them that every traveler we meet on the journey is a teacher for us and that each of us is climbing a mountain of our own challenges, conquering our own fears, and growing in wisdom in this lifetime.

As we closed our session, each woman pulled her final word for the program and read all eight of her words. We remarked at how each woman's set of words reflected her process.

After everyone left, Lily stayed behind and asked me what I thought her last word might mean: "Passage: A rite of passage will move you forward into new realms." Lily and I talked about her life and how in some ways she was at a passage point. She told me she knew she was leaving behind an old way of life and moving through a new gateway. She was excited at what she was learning, and just as important, she was happy to be part of a community of people who wanted to change their lives as much as she did.

I suggested that she pause and bless all that was in her past, that she imagine herself having come to an actual gateway on her journey. She could stand at the gate opening, glance back over her shoulder, and bless it all. Everything had brought her to this moment. Once she blessed it, she could step into a new territory now or, as her card had said, "move forward into new realms."

"I Am the Light of the White Feather."

Receiving the gift bag at the end of a program was always special for each person. In addition to the Heartliving heart pin, each bag contained a different quote that had been shared during the program, and each participant decided why she might have randomly chosen that bag and that quote inside in order to explore its meaning in her life. Ten quotes were shared to remind us of our new concepts, and I watched as Lily opened the scroll tucked in her bag and shared her quote with the group:

> With everything that has happened to you, you can either feel sorry for yourself or treat what has happened as a gift. Everything is either an opportunity to grow or an obstacle to keep you from growing. You get to choose. (Wayne W. Dyer[15])

---

[15] "Wayne W. Dyer > Quotes > Quotable Quotes," Goodreads, accessed March 18, 2019, https://www.goodreads.com/quotes/30189-with-everything-that-has-happened-to-you-you-can-either.

Lily said she knew exactly why she had chosen this bag. It could be easy, she said, to feel sorry for herself. She had done that early on with her first diagnosis. Yet she knew, she told us, that there was no power in that. She wanted to grow, she was choosing growth, and she was aware that the gift of her illness was the value she was placing now on being alive.

Several women told Lily how much they had seen her transform. When they first met her, one woman named Karen remarked that Lily had seemed quiet and tended to dismiss herself. In just eight short weeks, Karen said she witnessed Lily blossom. Lily looked at her with delight and smiled.

The women reflected to one another the beauty of each woman's process and how love, faith, and even sorrow and understanding had been birthed in these eight weeks. Spirits were high, and I could tell that no one wanted the meeting to end.

I decided it was time to give each woman the closing gift: a heart pin that was created by a local artist, a pin I had always given each graduate of the Leading from the Heart program. This evening, each woman received her heart pin and put it on immediately. As they sat in the circle together, I shared the story of how the pin was created.

"From the origin of my Heartliving programs, I had wanted to give each graduate a symbol of connection to our heart community. I had gone to jewelers everywhere, searching for a special pin that would represent that spirit. It was fate when I entered a boutique and a beautiful gold heart pin caught my eye. I tingled when I picked it up and held it. Artistically, the pin seemed to capture and symbolize the spirit of Heartliving. The boutique owner said the pin was one of a kind, made by a local artist, Anna Rosen. While she could not give me Anna's contact information, she was hopeful that I could find it. I proceeded to search for Anna but was unable to find her."

I could feel my body beginning to tremble as I spoke, an enormous energy building in my chest. I had shared this story many times, and I never tired of recalling the sacred experience. Yet it was never easy to overcome my emotion to share it.

I took a deep breath and continued. "Shortly after, a woman named Martina came to see me at the university. She noticed the gold heart pin I was wearing, and to my surprise, Martina knew the artist. What Martina shared, though, was even more important. Her daughter and Anna's daughter, Leah, had been in school together until fourth grade, when Leah developed a tumor that wrapped around her heart. It was inoperable, and in a short time, the young child passed away."

I saw tears brimming in Lily's eyes as I spoke. A chill came over me. I told the class that when Martina told me about Leah, I knew more than ever that Anna must make their heart pins.

"The next Saturday, I drove to Anna's home and showed her my logo. Anna was a petite woman, quiet, and very kind and unassuming. The artwork in her home was eclectic: modern paintings with broad, colorful strokes, classic sculptures of museum quality, and art nouveau lamps amid knickknacks from different countries. No mention was made of Leah, and Anna warmly assured me she could create the pins from my logo, ready in time for the last class."

At that moment, I stopped the story to wipe the tears from my eyes. I was shaking. A dear woman, Dolores, reached over and handed me a tissue. Soon the box was being passed around the circle. I took a sip of tea, collected myself, and went on. "That night after meeting with Anna, I went to bed rather late. In the middle of the night—I'm not sure why—I awoke suddenly from deep sleep to the sensation of light coming through the window, moving about on the floor. I sensed a spiritual presence in the room, and immediately and still half-asleep, I said to the spirit, 'Leah, your mother is making my heart pins. How will I know you?'" I have often spoken in intuitive moments without knowing what prompts my words.

"Leah's message came immediately into my consciousness with an answer I will never forget: '*I am the fractured light that comes through the window and dances on your floor. I am the light of the white feather.*'"

I told the class that as Leah delivered this message, I could feel my heart swell to the size of the room. I was instantly in a state of pure peace. I lay there calmed by an energy I have never since been fully able to experience again or to describe. When I awoke in the morning, I recalled the heart feeling and felt in awe of the experience.

As I was leaving for work and getting into my car, my eight-year-old daughter was standing at the front glass door. It was a ritual we shared each morning. As I looked through the car window at her, we waved and blew each other a kiss. I put the key in the ignition. In perfect position on the windshield right in front of my view, I could not miss a tiny white feather. I remembered Leah's words: "I am the light of the white feather!"

I took the tiny white feather off the windshield and felt dazed. *What does the white feather mean?*

Driving to the university, I thought about Leah. I could not imagine how tragic it must have been for her parents. I thought about her all morning as I went about my office work. On my lunch break, I was coaching a friend Angelique, who had just returned from Greece. She shared gorgeous photos with me and, before leaving, handed me none other than a magnificent white feather. She had been at a lake in Greece, and she told me that swans were everywhere. She had thought of me and wasn't sure why but wanted to bring me a white feather. The white feather, she had learned while in Greece, was a signature of an angel nearby.

As I continued sharing, I noticed the women sitting in the circle, all wearing the heart pin, each pin similar but not exactly alike. I reflected on their kindred hearts. I was so grateful that Lily was among them.

I told them that when I picked up the pins from Anna, I debated sharing the dream of Leah I had experienced. I didn't want to be intrusive or to upset her in any way. I asked Leah in my mind to help me know what to do.

Anna had laid the heart pins out beautifully on a royal-blue cloth. Each one was molded from clay, layered in the colors of the heart logo. Tiny gold hands were imprinted in the clay in different ways, with no two heart pins exactly alike.

"Imagine my surprise," I told them, "when Anna said to me, 'Cynthia, I know you don't know about my daughter, Leah, who passed away from cancer, but I think she had something to do with you finding the heart pin. She loved to draw hearts, especially ones with curved tails like your logo. The morning I created the gold pin you found, I felt her presence with me.'"

The women, especially Lily, were attentive to every word. Lily was wearing her heart pin on her shirt and had placed her hands over it, her fingers touching the pin throughout the story. Now Lily began to cry openly, and several women near her reached their arms out toward her, placing their hands on her shoulders. We were all quiet, women dabbing their eyes with tissue.

There was silence, and then Lily spoke through a trembling voice. "Leah is an angel. I don't know why she had to go, but Leah has a purpose on the other side. And, Cynthia, she found you ... and she found us." Asa, who had befriended Lily earlier, hugged Lily and thanked her for her insight.

The women together decided they were now part of the "white feather society." I told them that heart sisters in groups before them have found white feathers at the most interesting life moments and just when they needed encouragement and support. They agreed that they would wear their pins proudly, each pin layered with color and tiny gold hands stamped into the clay ... no two hearts alike, just like their own.

In the dim light as the candle burned brightly, Lily suggested we stand around the candleholder and create the same group hug. And as we stood there with our heart pins on, arm in arm, hearts open, I guided them through our closing meditation. We imagined the abundant world joining through our connectedness, while we made our requests with complete faith and trust in a goodness that we knew we were worthy of.

May Her Heart Be Safe

I noticed Lily approaching as I glanced out the office window. I opened the door to greet her, and she reached out to hug me. "Lily, I'm excited that we'll do some energy work today. Does a Reiki[16] session feel right for you?"

Lily nodded. "Yes, I want to see what you notice in my energy field. I was doing okay last week, but you know, after class ended, I was so sad for several days."

"Endings can create that kind of sadness, especially the ending of a class in which you've shared so much. It's like the class becomes a family."

Lily agreed, and then her words rushed in. "Oh, Cynthia, I just felt so connected in the class. I mean I know I can be in other classes, too, and I'll see some of the people again, but it was so good to look forward to being together each week."

Lily was eager to share. "Sometimes, especially at night, I get so afraid. And I don't even know what I'm afraid of. I just want to belong to something that's good."

---

[16] "Learn about Reiki, Definition of Reiki," International Association of Reiki Professionals, accessed March 17, 2019, https://iarp.org/learn-about-reiki/. Reiki is a Japanese hands-on healing method.

"I understand, Lily. I do." Lily leaned her head on a pillow on the couch. I could tell her chest was tight. She seemed to be holding her breath.

"Lily, take your time. We're in no rush. Let's talk a bit," I offered. "And we'll still have time for some energy healing. Tell me a little more about the feeling you've expressed about needing to belong." I knew that Lily was at an important juncture in her process. Her experience in the group was new to her, she had felt connected, and I didn't want her to disconnect, not from others and not from herself.

"Well, since my first diagnosis, I have felt that I haven't belonged in this world. My life isn't like everybody else's. People are in relationships, going about their lives, and I have been just trying to live. I don't know if I can fit in. I always wanted a relationship, but why would someone want me?"

Lily began to cry, dabbing small tears at first, and then her chest heaved with sobs. I reassured her. Then I remained silent, offering her the space to release her sadness.

As I watched her, my own eyes glistened with tears. "Lily, I'm right here." I pulled my chair closer and placed my hand on her back. What could I possibly say to comfort her? To tell her she was beautiful, to tell her she was enough, would seem insufficient. I let her know that I was here and that I would always be here. Most important, I needed her not to abandon herself.

Lily's face was buried in her hands, her back trembling. I could barely make out her words. "I just … want … to belong." When she cried, there was a rawness as though the wound of her aloneness had opened up. As much as she tried to hold it in, her muffled sobs released the deep sorrow that she had held inside herself for so long.

We talked about the cancer, how she felt she had belonged in the world before she had cancer. She had many friends then and a boyfriend whom she spent so much time with. After the diagnosis, she said, he eventually left her. So she focused on her animals and herself, doing what she loved, gardening, spending time with her family. Still, she said, she always just wanted someone to love her for herself.

I realized how much being with the heart sisters in classes had made her feel connected and cared for, understood, and a part of a community. She didn't want the closeness and connection to end.

I remembered my own devastation when I was left to raise two young children, ages one and five. I lived in a small two-story bungalow that I had purchased with my husband before our second child was born. After he left us, I would put the children to bed at night and be unable to enter my own bedroom. For the longest time, each night I sat at the top of the stairs on the landing in the dark as a small purple lamp in my bedroom created shadows on the walls. I felt as though I were keeping watch over a dead body, mourning the relationship that had ended abruptly. I remember endless days in which I would ride around, running errands with my children in the back seat, tears streaming down my face as I drove, hoping they would not see them.

There were so many moments in which I tucked them in at bedtime and read them stories, and I would notice their tiny shoes, their clothes that I had neatly arranged on the chair for the next day. There never seemed to be time to hold them long enough, to reassure them that they were loved and would always be loved, and never enough time for me to evidence my own sadness and fear.

No relatives lived near me. I had to be responsible for my family, to keep everything intact. Responsibilities were overwhelming at home and at work. I was a faculty administrator at a university. One morning after taking the kids to school, I pulled up at work, and as I reached for my briefcase to start my day, I was suddenly overcome with grief, exhaustion, and emotional pain. Months of sadness and disappointment came pouring in. I felt I was going to fall down in the parking lot. At that moment, I pushed everything back, deep into my cell tissue, and stood up straight with my briefcase in hand and walked into my building. I could not fall apart. There was no time to feel my pain. It wasn't until later that I was able to feel it with the help of a caring practitioner.

As I looked down at Lily, I wanted to be sure she was given the opportunity to release her pain. Her head was still in her hands, the pillow under her chest. She had ceased sobbing, but I remained silent until she sat up and spoke.

"Cynthia, I'm afraid of relationships. You know the guy I mentioned in class. Well, I like Mason, and we've been spending more time together. He can be nice, but …"—she hesitated to search for the right words—"sometimes he scares me. He yells over what seems like nothing."

"Lily, is there something in particular, in addition to the yelling, that he does that makes you uncomfortable?" I felt worried. I was concerned that Lily might be in a relationship with someone who was abusive.

"Well, he gets impatient with me sometimes." She hesitated and then continued, "I mean he says he really loves me, and I believe him, but he can have a short temper over what feels like stupid stuff. So it gets confusing."

"I see what you mean. That would be confusing, so let's try to figure it out." More than anything, I wanted Lily to be safe.

"Well," Lily hesitated, "Mason has highs and lows. I mean his moods can change quickly. And he is temperamental at times."

"I understand, Lily. That would be difficult." I knew Lily was fragile, emotionally and physically. She needed all her energy in order to be well, and she needed her energy exchanges to be loving. Stress and fear weakened the immune system. Knowing that her mental state contributed to her body, I wanted to protect her from emotional and physical trauma.

"But I think he means well, Cynthia. I do love him. I guess Mason and I are learning about love. I really feel like he's trying, even when what he does scares me."

Lily looked away from me toward the window. I recognized how difficult it was for her to be so vulnerable and knew she was desperate to be in a loving relationship. "I mean I want to trust him, but it's hard with his mood swings. A couple of times in the past month, he said he was coming over, and he didn't show up. He didn't call until a whole day later." Lily paused. There was a silence in the room.

"You know, yesterday, I had a fight with him, and he said some mean things. I told him to leave. I had to, and after I did, I felt better. But then he left, and I was alone again."

I felt more and more concerned about Lily's ability to discern whether Mason was safe. "Lily, is there something more you want to tell me?"

Lily's eyes filled up as if she were going to sob again. I knew she needed to tell me about something that was deeply bothering her. I allowed her time to gather herself, and after several moments, she said, "Cynthia, he hangs around with people who scare me. I'm afraid he might get into trouble."

"Lily, it's important to honor your feelings and to be careful to take care of yourself. You need to be safe. If for any reason, you are not comfortable around Mason, you can speak up or leave the situation. Most of all, you don't have to stay in a relationship that scares you."

Lily looked at me knowingly. I noticed her hands were shaking. I asked her if she needed a few moments. She nodded, and I guided her through a few deep and slow breaths until she felt calmer. We talked about how she deserved to love and protect herself and that she needed to be with someone she could trust. She was worth everything.

I could see that she felt more at ease. She was sitting upright and had placed her tissue next to her.

"Lily," I shared, "it's important to be good to yourself. I know you are good to others, and you deserve to expect the same in return. Just know that I'm always here if you are afraid or need to talk. We want you to stay healthy in your body, mind, and spirit. You deserve that."

Lily nodded her head, and I asked her, "How is your body feeling now?"

"I'm okay. Maybe the Reiki session will help."

Lily and I climbed the stairs to the treatment room. My office had the spaciousness of high ceilings that gave it a light and airy feeling, with low-hanging chandeliers that provided a cozy charm.

Once in the treatment room, I turned on golden tree lights in the corner of the room. The red curtains and purple walls were a beautiful contrast as the sunset gently filtered into the room. I turned on a flute instrumental, and Lily seemed relaxed within minutes of getting on the massage table.

As I gently performed the session, I noticed several energetic images and symbols that I was happy to share with her after her treatment: her majestic seagull flying effortlessly over choppy water; a spirit who seemed to want to make contact, one I had not noticed before, who, as Lily later told me, described her grandmother who had passed; and other meaningful images that she told me added a richness to her understanding of what she was learning in this lifetime.

The World Is So Connected

My next to last morning in Japan has arrived, and I am eager to go home. I am worried about Lily and don't understand why she has not been responding to my calls. Although my heart is heavy, I know I need to be present fully in Japan, yet she is constantly on my mind.

Shiori-san and I have a special day today. We are invited to a geisha house this evening, and I will do individual sessions with several women there, and we will enjoy a meal together.

We arrive at the house. Granite stones lead up to the front door, which is painted dark purple. Gorgeous gold star lights are strung across the porch ceiling and over the door. Immediately, I think of the inside of Lily's heart box. Her painted stars against a purple sky inside her heart.

We ring the bell, and Emi-san, a well-known geisha in Japanese theater, answers the door. Her perfect white teeth, powdered face, and bright red lips are a perfect contrast to her dark hair. She is wearing a mint-green kimono decorated with small white flowers and silver leaves. She has a fresh look. Shiori-san has told me that the geisha create a life of beauty. They are the embodiment of refinement in Japanese culture and present as living works of art.

We bow to each other, even though I have been told that as the sensei (teacher), I am not required to bow. Emi-san has invited me to provide energy readings to a group of geisha who are familiar with my benefactor in Japan. I had met Nakamura-san, a well-known, wealthy Japanese businessman, by chance years before when I was invited to Japan to perform energy readings. Through friends of mine who knew him, I was introduced and asked to perform a reading for him, and I did so. He was highly impressed with my skills and decided to sponsor my continued work in Japan so that people connected to him could benefit from my intuitive assistance.

Emi-san suggests that I work first with a young woman named Yui-san, who is considered a geisha in training. Her face is painted white, her dark hair jeweled with shiny combs in perfect position, her kimono held in place by a kimono belt that has coral and pearls inlaid in the silk material. Shiori-san explains to Yui-san how I do a session, and so I begin.

I have worked with many people in Japan on numerous trips before, and only several times have I been offered the privilege of working with geisha. Shiori-san instructs Yui-san to lie on the massage table, fully clothed with a sheet draped over her body and tucked up under her chin. I stand next to her and relax and tune in to her energy. I breathe calmly and allow the outer world to be suspended. An energy reading is something I have been trained to give and have done for years now. It is always a welcomed opportunity for me to assist others with what feels magical to me.

As I suspend my outer thoughts and tune in to my client's energy, I see certain intuitive images naturally appear. I begin speaking about these images that Yui-san says are completely clear to her—an old man whose initial is that of her grandfather who has passed on years before; the number five, which she tells me was the age of a trauma she experienced during a family outing and that has taken a lifetime for her to heal from; an image of a bear, which symbolizes the need for introspection, among other images. I discuss these and other impressions with her and help her weave an understanding about her life, the images creating a theme to help her, not unlike a waking dream.

When Shiori-san asks if Yui-san has any questions that she wishes to mention to me, Yui-san holds her head down and softly asks a question that Shiori-san translates: "Sensei, will I ever in this lifetime find true love?" I nod and smile to let her know that her question is understood. *This is my own question*, I think, as she glances up and her eyes meet mine. Like Lily on the other side of the world and souls of every culture, Yui-san's life goal is simply to love and to be loved.

I continue performing readings for three more women, and then our dinner is presented to us while the women I have read for individually perform through music and dance. We sit on the floor on cushions at a traditional low dining table. While the women sit cross-legged, I sit with my legs to one side, shifting often to avoid the numbness that sometimes sets in. I'm always grateful they understand.

Our traditional Japanese meal emphasizes variety and balance. It is achieved through color, cooking technique, and flavor. The aesthetic presentation of food is highly prized in Japan.

We are served plates of sashimi (raw fish), sushi (bite-sized meat, seafood, and vegetables wrapped in rice and seaweed), yakitori (bite-sized cuts of grilled meat), tempura (battered and fried vegetables), and udon (dense and chewy noodles made from wheat). Our meal begins and ends with *tsukemono* (traditional pickles that are made with a wide variety of ingredients, including radish and eggplant). What a delightful last evening in Japan with such gracious people!

It's time for Shiori-san and me to say our goodbyes, and we begin our walk back to her family home. Japanese lanterns are glowing on certain porches, some hanging from trees in the yard. As we walk back, I reflect on how our souls connect with one another often through our questions and unfinished stories. In this way, we contribute to one another's soulful evolutions. Some connections lead us to deep worlds within us, and for that, I am grateful.

As we walk back, I am again absorbed in my thoughts about Lily. I have been able only temporarily to suspend my worry. Once back in my room, I will try to call again. I'll pack everything up, and tomorrow I will head for Nagoya Airport to begin the journey back home.

I'm eager to make my call. Yet, for the third day in a row, Lily does not answer. I am deeply concerned and unclear, thinking maybe she is on a new pain medication or sleep regimen. I send yet another email and leave a voice mail as well. "Lily, I will be home on Monday evening, so I will call when I make my connecting flight in Detroit. I can't wait to see you. Until then, I hope you are well and remember I will be there soon. I love you."

I awake early to pack my bags carefully. Many beautiful Japanese gifts need to be packed, so I roll the clothes neatly to optimize space. My heart is always bittersweet about leaving my dear friends. After hugs and goodbyes, I board the long flight. The trip seems forever this time. My heart is troubled. What if something has happened to Lily? What if I am too late? I am unable to sleep, with lights turning on around me, then off, then on again. People are up and down in the aisles on this thirteen-hour flight. A baby is crying. I find it impossible to sleep.

Finally, we arrive in America. I wait for the heavy suitcases and then get through customs, anxious to turn my phone on in America and to call Lily. But time is short in between connections, so I must race to the last gate for my flight home. Many people are moving in different directions. I try to focus, but my body is exhausted and numb. I finally make it to the last gate. Anxiously, I call Lily, and there is no answer. The same message is still on her voice mail. I leave a message and board the plane heavyhearted.

When I arrive home and turn the phone back on, I have a text from Lily. My relief turns to shock as I read the message: "Hello. Lily is no longer taking messages on her phone and no longer able to have visitors. You may send a written note if you wish to the address below, but we feel it is best that she not have too much outside contact now. She is at her home resting peacefully. We appreciate your concern."

I am stunned. *I cannot speak to Lily? Is she okay? What has happened so suddenly?* I text back, trying to explain who I am. No response.

Once at home, I immediately write a note and drive it to the nearest mailbox:

> Dearest Lily, PLEASE ask someone to read this message if you cannot read it yourself. This is Cynthia. I am Lily's life coach and energy practitioner who has worked with her for nine years. She has asked me, and I have promised her, that I will be with her to continue supporting her through her challenging illness. I have been in Japan and have had trouble reaching her. Whoever can, would you please call me on my cell at 797-459-1066? I promised Lily that I would help her, and I believe she will want me there. I also understand any need for family privacy. I anxiously await your call.

"When the Time Comes, I'm Going to Be Okay."

It was late summer, and most of the students, Lily included, had requested a new workshop called "Ideas about the Afterlife." I would blend insights from my work in Japan and in Europe as well as from my education and my own experiences. Awareness of the unknown and of what occurs after death was of interest to many who were caring for aging parents or who had experienced illnesses themselves.

I began the workshop that day by sharing the conversation I'd had with Tanaka-san in Japan. They were fascinated with the idea of the overwhelming sense of freedom that the person who dies feels as well as the idea that our consciousness continues on the other side.

"Do you think we'll all be together on the other side?" Candice, an outgoing young woman, new to our programs, questioned. "We're all learning new concepts together. Personally, I'd love that!" Others nodded and thought how cool it would be to meet up again. I saw Candice smile at Lily, and Lily blushed and smiled back.

Tina, an engineer in her fifties, shared an experience she'd had with her mother, who was beginning hospice care. "I think my mother is really afraid and doesn't know what to expect. It's not that she hasn't lived a pretty good life, but I just feel that nothing has prepared her to understand what will happen when she passes. The other day," Tina continued, her voice quivering, "my mother asked me to help her understand what passing might be like. I guess I'm just really scared because I want to help her, but I don't know what to say." Tina was a quiet-spoken, refined woman who always spoke with a depth of feeling and was dedicated to her family. We all nodded our heads in understanding.

"I'm sorry, Tina. I'm hoping some ideas may help you with your mother. So, if it should happen, for example, that your mother would pass suddenly or unexpectedly, she might take comfort in knowing that it's believed that spiritual helpers will come to her before her actual death to guide her to the next dimension. In fact, many religious traditions teach that we meet each other again in the afterlife. It's possible that your father or other loved ones who passed before her will greet and help her."

"It would be very comforting for her to know that," Tina said.

"You know, I really believe that often we worry that we will say too much or something wrong to the person who is passing, but honestly, it may be very comforting to talk about what is going on. You can use your own intuition about this."

Jaeda spoke up and shared, "Cynthia, I'm glad we're talking about this, and I hope, Tina, it does relieve you because I think the responsibility of assisting another person is extremely hard. May I share what happened when my dad passed?" Jaeda was a middle-aged woman who had worked for years as a massage therapist. She had a depth and gentleness of spirit that we all admired. I knew that she and Lily went to the coffee shop together often, and Lily told me she had found such comfort in their conversations. Jaeda was someone Lily said she could open up to; her warm smile and kindness were uplifting.

"Sure, Jaeda. Please."

"Well, my father died in the nursing home and had been there for three years. He had a degenerative disorder that over time made him unable to feed or take care of himself. I remember that we had discussed in our heart class back then that the other side was vibrational." Jaeda looked at me with a questioning face. I nodded, and she continued, "And we also said that the afterlife dimension has been thought to run parallel to our world, so instead of being zillions of miles away, it is actually possibly right here but just not visible to us because of our limited vision."

"Exactly," I affirmed.

"Well, I shared those ideas with my father, and it really helped him when I explained to him that the world itself is completely vibrational in all dimensions."

Jaeda's long, dark hair beautifully framed her face, and her eyes were wide and full of emotion as she continued, "And I remember the afternoon he passed. I was with him, and I gave him a crystal to hold. I put it in his hand and wrapped my hand around his." She paused to gather her emotions. "Dad had lost all physical mobility and his sense of touch, and the crystal seemed to give him a new feel, a new touch. I told him that the afterlife was just a new dimension which he hadn't felt yet, but that he would go to, and that he would be able to feel again. I mean feel completely. Most important, I told him we would not really be separated at all. I told him I knew that different dimensions can coexist at different vibrational levels in the same space and that our hearts would always be together." Jaeda paused, looked down, and continued in a broken voice, "I remember watching him, the crystal in his hand and my hand over his, and I felt that at that moment he was more hopeful and alive than he had been in a long, long time."

There was a long silence in the room and a deep recognition of the truth and beauty of Jaeda's story. It appeared that what she shared had touched Lily deeply. Lily remarked, "I think assisting another person to feel safe is one of the most loving things we can do for each other." I thought of Mason and how much she needed to feel safe and secure.

We all agreed.

I went on to share something I learned in Japan, thinking it might be helpful to ease a person's anxiety. "In Japan, many believe that right after the soul is said to arrive on the other side, if the soul has suffered illness, especially for a long time or is depleted, the soul is said to stay between an earthly world and the spirit realm for a period of time to recover, after which the soul is told which level of the other world they will go to." Discussion ensued as we spoke about one another's loved ones who had passed and how helpful it was to think that they would have received such loving care and direction.

Evelyn, a nurse who was knowledgeable and compassionate, spoke up. "You know, Cynthia, before my mother passed, she wondered about whether she would go through a life review. What are your thoughts on that?"

"That's an important question. You know, many times people have been taught that they'll be judged, often from religious upbringing. I understand from my reading and from lectures I've attended that no harsh judgment takes place, not as we think of judgment on earth. We are said to be evaluated on how well our souls acted upon our life roles and learned lessons with love."

I noticed that Lily had been listening intently, taking pages of notes. At this moment, she spoke up. "The life review really is interesting to me. I think during our lives we often look back on stuff and choices we made and kind of do a life review as we go. But this life review after our death sounds like, when it happens, you see your life from a viewpoint different than your own."

"Well said, Lily. It's often taught that souls will see and feel not only what they experienced while being alive but will understand how others were affected by their words and actions too. They will know the effect they had on others."

Lily seemed pleased and much more relaxed. She had tucked her shoes under the table and pulled her feet up under her. Her notepad was on her lap, and she leaned her elbow on the arm of the couch. I noticed how calm she seemed amid the intensity and engagement with others. Perhaps they were all focusing on certain people or circumstances they had encountered. Would knowing that others would see the effects of their behavior make it easier to forgive?

Courtney, a communications trainer who had a cute sassiness about her but was always invested in depth discussion, opened her hands, lifted them up, and reflected out loud, "So I guess ultimately, it appears that all things during our lifetime become clear to each of us when we pass. So, I think you're saying, Cynthia, that you are your own judge, yet you work with spiritual guides who help you assess your life and gain greater understanding. Does that sound right?"

"Yes, Courtney, nicely said. And that fits with what Lily was saying about our life review as a time for us to learn how we might have affected others."

A kind woman, Diane, shared a touching story about her brother and how much she had loved him, feeling that they had been through many lifetimes together. "I've always wondered if there are ways for us to know that our loved ones who've passed are nearby. It's been years since my brother passed, but I still get feelings that he is around me."

Others nodded their heads in agreement about their own loved ones. We discussed ways we thought the souls might let us know they were around; then I shared some traditional ways that it is believed souls can tell us they are present: lights may flicker, electronic devices may turn on or off randomly, the smell of cologne or even cigarette or pipe smoke may be evidenced, pets' behavior may seem unusual, and even room temperature may feel cooler.

"Is it possible," Marie, an elementary school teacher, asked, "that you may have a sense that someone is watching you, but no one is physically around?"

Lily nodded in agreement and added, "Or you feel as if someone has touched you?"

Lily told us she often felt, when she was young, that a relative who passed had been around her. One time she said she was sitting on a couch and had a feeling that someone had sat down beside her, yet no one was physically there.

We continued to weave an understanding of the afterlife, to know that we are all connected, that life is full of opportunities for each of us to exercise freedom of will and choice, while ultimately, we are here to grow and to learn love together.

As the class members were leaving that day, Lily took me aside. "This workshop helped me a lot, Cynthia. I'm not as afraid of dying anymore. I have a bigger picture now. When the time comes, I'm going to be okay. Of course, I still want to live," she said shyly, "but I know there's really nothing to be afraid of. And just like my word that I drew from the box today said, Cynthia, I'm healing."

17

My Heart Leapt for Joy

When I returned home from Japan, I was back in the office two days later, still experiencing jet lag and seeing just a few clients at first. Most of all, I was waiting for a response to my note I had mailed to Lily, and I was worried.

That afternoon there was a message on my phone from Lily's sister, Colette: "Hi, Cynthia. Lily got your card today. She's still conscious, but she's in bed now and unable to walk without assistance. She's conserving her energy as much as she can. I did read your note to her, and she asked me to tell you to please come. It's been so busy here with getting her care lined up."

My heart leapt for joy! *Lily is alive, and I can see her.* I had been so worried. I called back immediately, and Colette answered. We agreed that I could see Lily at four o'clock. Colette explained that I would enter an outer door to Lily's building and come up to the third floor. I was to knock softly, and someone would let me in. Although my relationship with Lily had spanned nine years, I had never been to her home.

I arrived at Lily's apartment door in an old Victorian-style building. The front door led into three units, one on each floor. I wound my way up to the top floor, and as Lily's sister had requested,

I knocked gently. I remember Lily saying that she had an older sister and brother.

Colette opened the door. Although her eyes were much like Lily's, her face seemed tired and guarded. I could only imagine how hard this time must be for her. I could sense the pain in her demeanor, yet I could still feel her kindness and gentle spirit.

I glanced around at the high ceilings, tasteful decor, spiritual art, well-tended plants, and family pictures. Lily's home was pleasing and warm.

An assistant from a nursing care company sat on the couch, recording notes about Lily's care and setting up a chart. She was middle-aged, with gray hair pulled up in a twist and dark eyes under tortoiseshell glasses. She had a stocky build and was wearing powder-blue scrubs and white nurse's shoes. She smiled as I shook her hand and introduced myself. "I'm Cynthia, Lily's life coach and friend."

"I'm Edith. Nice to meet you. Lily's a sweet girl. We're setting up her care plan and trying to keep her comfortable. Want to have a seat?"

"Sure. Is it okay to see her?" I hesitated. "Of course, whenever it's appropriate. I don't want to disturb her."

"Yes, sure. Let me check. I can take you back to her room."

I followed Edith as we wound our way down a hallway to the back of the house. I was moved to see Lily's Heartliving certificates framed and hanging in the hallway. Her heart box sat on a small hall table next to statues of Mary and the Buddha. As we turned one bend, a cat dashed past us. "Oh," Edith said, "that's Spirit. Lily told me she found Spirit outside a few years ago by chance and put up photos, but no one came forward. So, Lily told me she guessed Spirit was supposed to be hers. She does love her critters."

Edith stopped at a doorway, and as I stood next to her, I could see Lily lying in her bed, her back to us. Another medical assistant motioned to us to wait a minute, having just given Lily a shot to ease the pain. I was overcome with emotion, and my heart pounded as I saw Lily turn her head slowly toward the door.

"Lily, you have someone here to see you." Edith spoke in a soft tone.

Lily's eyes squinted, and she seemed to have trouble seeing. "Lily, it's Cynthia," I whispered.

Her face softened, and a smile came over her face, her eyes opening more fully. "Oh, Cynthia. I've missed you!"

"Lily, I've missed you so much. I'm home now." The nurse motioned for me to sit in the chair by her bed. I took Lily's hands in mine.

Lily was sedated, and her speech was slow at first. Her eyes seemed to float in and out of a dreamy state as though she could see but not clearly. Her face was pale. There were medical supplies on the end table next to her bed.

"It's in my bones, Cynthia," she whispered. "I know you told us that parts of the body represent things. But I can't remember what bones represent."

"Bones, Lily, stand for the soul ... Ligaments, muscles, and tendons are the mind. The fluids are the emotions." I squeezed her hands gently. "The bones are the soul."

"That's right," Lily offered slowly. Maybe it was the pain medication or just sheer exhaustion from her illness that made her so weak. "Cynthia, you told us sometimes a person falls and breaks a hip before dying. It's their soul preparing them to go home." I wanted so much to console her, to give her the strength to continue.

"Lily, honey, your soul is taking care of you." I could feel a lump in my throat as I pushed back my emotion.

"I want to ask about all the stuff that happens when we go. No one here knows what we talked about before. Help me remember." Her voice was soft but pleading.

"Of course, Lily. Of course," I reassured her.

"It makes me not so afraid."

"I understand." The medical assistant and Edith had left the room. Edith glanced back and nodded her head, letting me know to take my time with Lily. I was so grateful to have the privacy and to know that I could help Lily understand in any way that she needed.

And so I talked gently and slowly with Lily, highlighting some of the points we had shared in our class on the afterlife. The possibilities of what might happen, remembering that most of all, she would be met by her loved ones—Mom, Dad, Grandma—and that she would not be alone, that she didn't have to perform or do anything when she passed. There was no need to worry. She would be guided safely and gently.

Lily told me her mother had promised that they would meet again on the other side, and she knew it was true. She also said Pop had told her he'd see her again. I nodded my head, reassuring her it was true.

I told her I understood she would be out of pain during her transition, maybe feeling lighter than she had ever felt. I asked her when was the lightest feeling she'd ever had, and she remembered a roller-coaster ride as a child when she said her heart seemed to be left at the top of the hill and her body so very light. I told her that the same lightness might come back but without any fear. Also, she said she felt light when she loved on her animals, that holding them did that to her.

I reminded her that her ancestors would greet her and how happy her reunion would be, and that at some point, she would review her life with kind spirit helpers who would cover the lessons she learned, going over what she did well and discussing with love and encouragement also what might have been better. No judgment, though, just all done in a loving way of learning and growing.

I mentioned that the universe in spirit is like a symphony of harmony so that she may hear beautiful sounds, feel expansive feelings, and again all of it very beautiful and soothing as she transitioned. Most of all, I encouraged her not to be afraid.

Lily smiled weakly. "I'm not afraid. I don't know why I am so calm, but I am." She closed her eyes and continued, "It was never really about the cancer, Cynthia. It was all about love and connection."

I reflected on all that Lily had been through, and my heart was overflowing with compassion and love for her. She had tried so hard and been so brave. She had wanted so much to heal, and I had tried so hard to give her hope.

I held her hand a little tighter. "Lily, you have learned so much and been so brave." I thought of our conversations, our many sessions and classes in which Lily shared her thoughts and feelings, her anxiety and her hopefulness. I couldn't bear to lose her, yet I was so grateful she was telling me she wasn't afraid. I felt deep down that Lily had come to a place in herself of acceptance.

I spent the rest of the afternoon into the evening with Lily, and in between small bouts of sleep, she would awaken and want to talk again. I stayed present, holding her hand and letting her know I was there, just as I had promised. She was not alone.

At one point, she became more energized, and her voice was stronger. "Cynthia, I know that a lot of stuff I worried about doesn't mean anything now." Lily's voice trailed off for a moment and then came back. "And you can't control what happens. Some things are bigger than you. And it's okay."

The crystals in her window sent beams of light on the walls and floor. There were moments of silence as Lily paused and reflected. "I'm glad I had this lifetime, and it helps me to know I have another chance."

"You have done so well, Lily." I noticed the trinkets and decorations in the room and felt at peace that the light illuminated pleasing images of angels and nature.

Lily was wearing a long, ankle-length cotton gown with a pattern of tiny blue flowers on a yellow background. Her hair was brushed back from her face. "I've been sick so much, trying to beat cancer each time. Remember when you told us it can be good to ask for guidance and to let go? I did that yesterday." Lily's eyes looked far away as though she was seeing into another dimension. She whispered, "I couldn't let go before."

I watched Lily's eyes close then open as she seemed to focus on something outside of the physical realm. I knew how often I had done this, especially as a child, when I began to see into other dimensions. I could tell she was seeing something that was not physically present. I added softly, "You are wise, Lily, to surrender and trust."

I watched her chest rise and fall, her breathing becoming a little more labored. "Cynthia, what is the thing about allowing?"

"About allowing? ... Well ..." I had to decide what I should say. I wanted to answer her questions but also wanted her to remain peaceful and calm. I knew she needed answers, yet I could tell talking seemed to make her tired. So I decided to speak to her gently and give her answers that might keep her from being afraid, as well as let her know I was physically present.

"When we allow, we are able to let go and surrender just like you've done. You know, Lily, I think in our lives, most of us try to stay in control. But it's good to allow spirit to guide us. That's what you're doing."

"Yes," Lily whispered. I was pleased at how gentle her energy seemed to be, and while I knew the pain medication was helping, I was also sure that all the work she had done and her level of trust in a greater good were contributing to her sense of peace.

At that moment, Colette poked her head in the door. "You have some mail today, Lily. Looks like some people are thinking of you. Maybe Cynthia can read your mail to you. Would you like that?"

I smiled at Colette as she gave me a handful of cards. There were five. I turned to Lily and continued gently, "Look at how many cards you have. Oh, here's one from Patricia, Bernie, Jennifer, and Raven, and here's one from Asa." Lily's face lit up with a smile. I realized she was not able to see the images or read the messages, so I read and described each card to her. We talked about how her friends were thinking of her and praying for her. She had tears in her eyes.

I hugged her and then arranged the cards on the mantel on either side of an art deco peacock that stood proudly in the middle. At the heart of the peacock was a clock, its face white with bold black numbers and delicate hands. "I really love this peacock, Lily. It looks so old."

Lily smiled as though she had a fond memory. "It was my mother's clock. I love it too."

"You know what the peacock stands for?" I asked her. There was silence. "Wise vision, Lily. All the eyes in the feathers are said to symbolize wise vision. Just like you have."

I sat next to Lily and began to feel her peacefulness. The sun was beginning to set, and I turned on the lamp. It created a beautiful glow that illuminated so many of her treasures. "You know you have so many interesting and sentimental things in your home. It's so cozy. I really love how you created this feeling it has."

"I've been here seven years now. It's my sanctuary, my safe place. I'm glad I'm not at the hospital. I'd rather be here." Lily seemed so sure of where she was and how glad she was to have arrived here.

"I'm so glad you're here too. It's so good that you have this safe place."

I was glad that Lily was not in a sterile room but in one that contained her fondest memories and treasures, a place she had created that brought her joy. Although grateful for her tranquility, I had begun feeling her impending death. As much as I wanted her to live, I was aware that she longed for freedom. I knew she would go to a dimension that would embrace her and free her of suffering, yet I was also aware that I would miss her physical presence dearly. Lily had become much like a daughter to me. I met an innocent and kind, gentle and unassuming young woman nine years before, one who suffered from an illness that she had no control over. I watched her mature into a woman who was learning to speak up for herself and was often wise beyond her years.

"Cynthia?" Lily took a deep breath, and her voice sounded stronger. "Why do some of us go through so much?"

"I'm not sure. I think hard lessons are chosen by very courageous souls." I looked down at Lily and could see that she was listening with her head cocked to one side. "Lily, you've moved so beautifully through your struggles, and you've learned so much. Remember we carry our understanding with us into the afterlife. Look at how smart you're going to be!" I noticed Lily's eyes were closed, but her lips had a little curve to them, a tiny smile, no movement in her cheeks, almost a sign of bliss.

Lily took another deep breath, and I could see tears now brimming in her eyes.

I gently held her hand and tried to hold back my own tears. I steadied my voice. I needed to remain strong for her. "And when we pass, we lose our physical body, but remember—your essence is never lost. Your body is simply a garment you wore during this lifetime. That's all. Your soul is much larger. Your soul is forever." I wanted so much for her to be at peace about passing. I wasn't sure why there were tears in her eyes. I trusted that she would let me know what she needed.

Suddenly, Lily said, "I remember now," and her tears rolled down her cheeks.

I squeezed her hand and remained silent. I wasn't sure what she meant. I wanted to give her the space to remember. Then after a few moments, I said softly, "Yes, Lily?" I dabbed her tears gently with a tissue.

Lily took another deep breath and asked me in broken speech, "Will ... will ... my family understand? They don't ... know what to expect." Lily worried about her world, about others, often more than about herself. I remember her telling me she just wanted to be connected, to know she belonged.

"I think they will be very sad, but they will remember and cherish all your times together. It's hard, Lily, when someone passes, but each of us will pass. You may pass before them, but they will pass too. And remember you can send messages to them."

Lily stretched her shoulders as though she were attempting to sit up in bed. "How should I send messages? Tell me again." Her voice was suddenly stronger.

I paused and tried to formulate my thoughts in an easy way for Lily to remember the ideas. "Well, you can do different things. Maybe you can turn lights on or off, or you can use a song on the radio as a message, or you can come to them in a dream. You will know what you can do when you get there. The angels and spirit guides will help you. And I'm sure Pop will share a few tricks with you!" Lily laughed faintly, but I knew any mention of Pop brought her joy.

"Most of all, once you have gone to the afterlife, you will be peaceful, and you can continue learning. Just remember the life of your soul will not end. Your soul is eternal."

I noticed that the light coming through the curtains was growing dimmer. The tapestry above her bed of Archangel Gabriel made the angel seem strong and confident. I prayed for Lily's confidence. Her eyes were opening a little more, and she looked around the room as though she were trying to get her bearings in her changing world.

"I want to continue learning. But I'm sad for my family."

I looked at this dear soul. I reminded her of the power of love and that they would always love one another. Lily squeezed my hand and looked away at the far window. Her eyes were beginning to close. She seemed to be relaxing again.

"Everything will be okay," I reassured her. Lily's breathing had become slower and more even. "And, Lily," I continued in a soft voice, "you don't have to remember any of this. You don't have to know what to do. Remember, you will be guided and loved. Instead of being so far away, you'll be right here, just in another dimension. We are always connected through our hearts."

Lily smiled and opened her blue eyes. They were weak with a redness around them. Her hair was matted around her forehead. She appeared to have suddenly remembered something and spoke up again. "You know, my grandmother came to me last night. She was in a white station wagon." Lily stopped as though trying to see the car. I assumed she was talking about a dream. "She never had a white station wagon, but she was in one. I thought she was going to take me with her, but she said I was still learning, and she would come back."

Lily paused, then continued, "And where she was driving, I could see light. Different layers of light all woven together, like threads and icy stuff. It was beautiful, like snowflakes."

I touched her hand gently. "That's beautiful."

CYNTHIA LYNCH BISCHOFF, PHD

"Yeah, and she said I might float through these layers to get to her, but she would look out for me and help me. And there would be music. I shouldn't be afraid of anything. Everyone would help me. Just like we learned."

My eyes filled with tears, and I felt a pressure in my chest. It was all I could do not to cry. I was so moved by her image and the support her grandmother was giving her.

Lily took another deep breath and continued, "She said after I passed, I might be healed for a little while at first."

I was speechless and so grateful that I could witness this beautiful soul, so courageous, so lovely.

"Lily, you are so brave. I know your grandmother will be right there to meet you. She'll help you to understand, and just as we learned, everything will become clear as you pass. I know it will be as she told you." I noticed how the light from the lamp was now illuminating her blonde hair, picking up the yellow in her gown. I felt she had turned a corner. She seemed to be more and more ready to leave, anticipating it without fear.

"Lily, some say there will be gorgeous colors, flowers, and objects there that we could never imagine here on earth."

Lily nodded. "Everything has a soul. The plants and flowers do too." Lily seemed to have found new strength and hope.

I thought about how wise Lily was, how much she had been through in so short a lifetime, how gentle her spirit. She opened her eyes and smiled, gazing at the ceiling as though she could see the flowers and their souls there.

"Cynthia, thank you for being in my soul group. I don't know what I would have done if … if I were to die without understanding." I could see Lily's chin trembling. She continued in a voice that sounded both shaky yet sure. "I think there are people who help others understand how it all fits together. These helpers are like angels or maybe … advanced souls." She turned her head and looked directly at me as though she could see me clearly. "I think that's who you are."

I was overcome with gratitude, finding it hard to speak. I swallowed and breathed deeply, trying not to cry. "Lily, I have loved helping you. With all you've learned, I think you are certainly an advanced soul too."

Lily smiled and closed her eyes again. The nurse came in to check her vitals, so I took the moment to go to the kitchen. Lily's sister was standing at the counter, taking notes and helping to set up the care plan. "How are you doing, Colette? May I help you with anything?"

"No, I'm fine. Cynthia, thanks for helping Lily."

"Thanks for letting me be here." Then I leaned in and whispered, "Colette, has the nurse said anything about Lily's condition or what to expect?"

"Not exactly." Colette's face looked drawn. I could sense a heaviness around her. "I'll ask her when she comes out with the latest on her vitals."

The nurse left Lily in the bedroom on the other side of the apartment and entered the kitchen to let us know that Lily was resting. She jotted down additional notes for the evening nurse before leaving. She finally had a moment to introduce herself to me. Jody shared that she would be working most days, starting on Monday. "It's hard to know how long it will be now," she said. "It could be several weeks or … less. Our goal is to keep her comfortable and in as little pain as possible. On Monday, we'll start round-the-clock care."

I looked at Colette and remembered I was off the next day. "I can be here tomorrow very early if that helps. What time works best for you?"

"Whatever time is best for you is fine," Colette said. "Do you want to text me when you get up?"

"Sure. I will probably be up by six thirty if that's not too early."

"Early is good."

Lily looked so much like her older sister. Although Colette was taller and her blonde hair was short and curly, her eyes carried the same intensity of feeling and depth. Her hesitations and posture let me know how worried she was and how much responsibility she had on her shoulders.

"Do You Love Me?"

Saturday morning came early, and I found myself waking up at six o'clock. I could see portions of an overcast sky as I glanced out the window, grabbing my robe to go downstairs. In addition to the jet lag from my trip to Japan, I was deeply troubled and had not slept well for several nights. Knowing I could spend the day sitting with Lily, helping Colette, and doing whatever was needed eased my heart.

This coming week would start the twenty-four-hour care, and I wasn't sure how much time Lily had left. I texted Colette at six thirty, and she said she would really appreciate my getting there early today, whenever I could, that someone was with Lily now but that she was going to pick up supplies and would be along quickly.

When I knocked at Lily's door, I heard a male voice answer from the hallway, "Come on in. It's not locked."

I could hear Lily talking with a man whose voice I didn't recognize. Then he called to me from the hallway, "Just a moment. I'm helping to prop Lily up in her bed."

"Hi. Take your time. I'm Cynthia, her friend."

"She'll be ready in a minute."

"Thanks. I'll wait here." I wondered who the male voice was.

CYNTHIA LYNCH BISCHOFF, PHD

From the back room, I could hear Lily speaking. "I love you, Mason. Do you love me?" Her voice was sweet and faint.

Mason? I remember now. Her boyfriend.

His voice was reassuring. "Baby, you're the sweetest, most beautiful woman in the world. Of course I love you." There was a softness to his voice.

Moments later, rounding the corner from the hallway, a middle-aged man appeared, wearing gray khaki pants and a dark sweatshirt, seeming slightly apprehensive.

"Hi, I'm Mason. Cynthia?"

I nodded, and he continued, "Colette said you were coming. I'm headed in to work this morning, so I need to get going. Lily wants you to come on back."

I followed Mason down the hallway and back to Lily's room. I thought of what she had told me, how she knew that she loved him but how she said he scared her at times, a little more abrupt than she was sometimes comfortable with. His voice was kind under the present circumstances, although he didn't smile or make eye contact with me.

As I entered the room, I saw Lily sitting up in bed. "Hey, Lily. I'm here early." I paused, waiting for her to see me. She was staring at Mason.

I continued. "I hope you rested well last night. It's Saturday, and I'll have more time to spend with you today." Lily seemed more animated than yesterday, as though she had a second wind.

"Did you meet each other?" she asked, motioning toward Mason.

"Yes, we just did." I watched how Lily looked sweetly at him.

"Cynthia," Lily said, "and Mason, I wanted you to meet each other." She turned toward me. "Cynthia, Mason has had a few slip-ups recently, but he just got a new job, and he's getting on his feet again." Looking again at Mason, she continued, "I know you can do it … and you can go to Cynthia if you need help."

I felt awkward but nodded my head yes.

Mason looked uncomfortable as Lily continued, "I know you can stay on track. Just please try hard, okay?"

"Lily, I will. I promise." Mason glanced at me, and his face turned red. He looked away and then turned toward me and said, "Since you're here, I'll head out so I can get in to work early."

"Okay, sure."

Mason sat on the edge of the bed, leaned over toward Lily, and whispered goodbye. Lily asked him if he would be coming back tomorrow, and he said he'd try to. He grabbed his backpack more quickly than I liked and headed out toward the front door.

Moments later, I could hear the door open again. Colette came in, gave Lily her meds, and within twenty minutes, Lily started falling asleep. This allowed me a few moments to chat with Colette.

Back in the living room, we sat on the couches. We discussed the now twenty-four-hour care starting on Monday. Colette said she or another family member would be staying all the time. I was welcome to stay with Lily too.

Even though I was listening to Colette, I was distracted. I felt worried. *"Mason, do you love me?"* I could hear Lily's question moments before. I was wondering whether Mason would come back after work. Did he love her? I remembered her telling me that she thought he meant well but that she found it hard to trust him with his mood swings. That several times he said he was coming over and didn't show up.

My heart was troubled. I worried about Lily's vulnerability. She had so much wanted to be connected and to be loved. Lily's words to Mason lingered in my mind: *"Just please try hard, okay?"* And his reply, *"I'll try. I promise."*

I Held Her Warm Hand in Mine

Monday morning started the full-time nursing care, and Colette texted me that Lily had asked when I was coming. I told her that I could come a little earlier that day, and we decided that two o'clock might be better. My last client, Patricia, was a dear friend of Lily's. I knew she would understand the cancellation. They had met in the classes and often had lunch together. "Please give her my love," Patricia said. "Tell her I'm praying for her." Patricia had the same gentle soul that Lily had, surely part of the same soul group, they often remarked.

I left the office rather quickly, knowing that every moment was precious. The street was lined with parked cars, causing me to have to walk a bit farther on this crisp fall day. The leaves were changing, another season coming. I could hear the words of my dear grandmother, "Such is life." Grandmother accepted life changes in the same way that she accepted seasonal changes.

Quickly I was inside the old building, winding my way up to the third floor. Today, I noticed even more beautiful details. Above Lily's apartment door was a transom window that seemed to catch just the right amount of light when I was inside. As Colette greeted me, I admired the ornately carved woodwork that adorned the living room. The fireplace mantel was painted white with a beveled mirror above it.

Even though papers had begun piling up on the side table alongside medical supplies, and some pillows were on the sofa and some sliding off, the front room remained magnificent and full of color—a purple velvet couch, a fuchsia-and-gold throw on the chair, knickknacks atop tables, and all types of pictures and small sculptures to please the eye.

"She's been waiting for you." Colette smiled.

"I was anxious to get here."

As we rounded the hallway, I saw the nurse, Jody, sitting by Lily's side. She smiled and said to me, "Cynthia, Lily was telling me how she had become a Reiki master. I mentioned to her that her hands always seem to be so warm. She told me it's her energy as she sends herself Reiki."

Lily glanced up at me as I entered the room. Her skin was pale and her eyes weak. Her lips appeared dry.

I reached down to kiss Lily's forehead. "Yes." I turned to the nurse. "Lily is highly skilled in Reiki. She has such wonderful energy."

Lily seemed a little further away today, her eyes half-open, not totally in this realm.

Jody stood up and smoothed Lily's blanket. "I'll let you two talk. I'll be right in the next room." Jody had a warm smile and a kindness that radiated from her. I was so glad that Lily's caregivers were such gentle souls.

"Thank you." I smiled. "Lily, how are you feeling today?"

She responded slowly, "I'm good," and feigned a weak smile. "I feel like I'm just floating. Maybe it'll be today that I go." Her voice trailed off as she closed her eyes.

"I know they're waiting for you when you're ready." *All in perfect order and in divine timing*, I thought, reflecting on how calm Lily seemed. I held her warm hand in mine, knowing that I would not always have the treasure of her physical presence. As she began to doze off, I allowed my consciousness to become softer and slower, releasing my own thoughts of loss and fear as I held an anchor for her in this world.

Glancing about the room, I admired all the beautiful touches of art and design that Lily had created. I thought of how delightful the physical realm can be, making it also sometimes hard to leave, and how many times throughout our lives we decorate and redecorate our space, our rooms, our lives, and … our hearts.

What if we could plan the journey our hearts take in the way that we plan a road trip? And what if we could look back on our heart's journey and honor the times we followed our map as well as the missed exits and the times we got lost? How often when I was young did I intend to create a certain life, hope for a certain outcome, instead to find that my life had seemed to create me?

How many times did Lily tell me that she desired to be well, to be loved? What if we could appreciate the contribution of all our life moments?

And what if, at some critical passage, we were able to see the journey from a sacred bird's-eye view, allowing us to witness a bigger picture? Wouldn't that change how often we fixate on the little things?

I remember Lily telling me in sessions that she had spent much of her life in search of love and approval, confiding that her energy often focused on pleasing friends, family, and partners. So many challenges occurred, and there were so many attempts to hold on. It wasn't until recently, she had told me, that she had begun to bring light into the dark places in herself, the places she had walled off to protect her sensitive spirit. She was proud that she had begun to express rather than to silence herself, to nurture herself rather than to deny her needs. It was when she knew she couldn't live forever and was no longer afraid to leave this world that, she confided, she had finally freed herself.

I was so proud of her, knowing that many of us never challenge our fears and rules about how the world works. How many times had I found a need to renegotiate certain life investments that had once seemed fulfilling but later seemed so empty?

As my thoughts trailed off, I felt a gripping of Lily's hand in mine. I glanced at her face, studying her, knowing I would never forget all she had taught me. Lily lay beneath her tapestry of the angel, whom she knew protected her. I sat beside her bed, thinking that Lily herself was an angel. I remembered learning that angels were not limited by time and space since they were said to exist as energy. *Yes, Archangel Gabriel,* I thought, *please keep a watchful eye over this dear soul.*

I had been taught that angels did not belong to a certain religion, nor were they concerned simply with people but with the environment and all animals as well. I had no doubt that angels were watching over Lily and would be there to guide her home.

I closed my eyes, feeling the warmth of Lily's hand, and noticed that she was drifting asleep. Suddenly, I felt the presence of someone coming into the room. I glanced at the doorway to see a man of large stature who appeared to be in his midforties, broad shouldered and tall with sandy hair and deeply set eyes. He introduced himself as Lily's brother, Andrew. His voice was deep, his smile friendly.

"Hi, I'm Cynthia, Lily's friend and life coach," I whispered as I stood up to shake his hand. "Please come in." I nodded at Lily, sleeping. "Here, take my seat, and I'll go into the front room. I know she'll be happy you're here when she wakes up." I stood up to exchange places with him. Andrew seemed like a gentle giant, as Lily had described him to me previously.

Once in the living room, I saw Colette resting on the couch. I could only imagine how hard it must be for her to take care of every detail, but most of all, to lose her only sister. *Please keep a watchful eye over this dear soul,* I thought.

I curled up into a chair in the corner, and for over an hour, I rested my eyes, my soul. I realized how little I had been sleeping these past few weeks.

An hour later, the nurse, Jody, came into the living room and said Lily was asking for Colette and me. As we walked into the bedroom, Andrew got up to exchange places with us.

Lily seemed more rested and a little stronger. I allowed Colette to take the chair Andrew had been in, and I stood on the left side of the bed. I had no idea what Lily needed us both for. Her voice was soft, her eyes still dreamy, and her breathing more shallow.

"Colette, you are my sister. I love you." Lily looked at Colette with a gentleness in her face.

"I love you, Lily." Colette took Lily's hand. Although she appeared to hold back her emotion as though trying to remain strong for Lily, her eyes were wet.

"Colette, I just want you to know that Cynthia is my heart sister and I love her too. You are both my sisters. I mean in different ways."

We both listened and nodded.

"I just want to be sure it's okay with you that Cynthia can be here any time and even at the end." She took a deep breath as though she were relieved.

As much as I loved Lily, I wanted to shrink, feeling that my connection did not compare to a lifetime that Colette had experienced as a sister to Lily. Still, I was moved that Lily was speaking up and wanting her requests to be known, and of course, I wanted to help her.

"Yes, it's fine for her to be with you. It's fine." Colette gave Lily a kiss on her forehead, then rose to return to the living room.

"Thank you, Colette," I offered.

Lily immediately started confiding in me with what seemed like a newfound intensity. "Cynthia, remember you helped me figure out why I was here in this lifetime? I don't remember now." She slowed down to take another deep breath. "What did I stand for?"

"I'll help you remember. Lily, what meant the most to you in this lifetime?"

Lily sighed. "Nature … animals … children … and harmony."

Suddenly, Lily made an unpleasant face as though she were about to cry. "But I never got married. I never had children. I didn't work much. I don't feel like I did anything." Her lips quivered, and I could sense what appeared to be her feelings of uncertainty about her life.

"Lily, you experienced more than most people do in a lifetime. You worked to understand your life. You're so kind to everyone and everything. That's more than most people can say they've done in a lifetime."

Lily smiled weakly. "I was thinking of the pearl necklace. I don't know what pearl I'm on. Can you help me to know?" I sensed that Lily was getting closer to the end, and while she seemed peaceful at times, she vacillated with anxiety about being enough, doing the right thing, making sure she was okay to leave. I could only imagine what she was going through. She was so brave.

"Let me help you, Lily. The pearl necklace is a symbol for the soul's evolution, how we're learning as we grow through our lifetimes. You know, when you think of a necklace of many pearls, none of us knows what pearl or lifetime we're on. Maybe we're on the tenth or the one hundredth." I paused to see if Lily was understanding. She seemed to be listening closely.

I continued, "In each lifetime while we are here on earth, we are learning how to love ourselves and each other. So we must trust that each lifetime is about learning." I paused and noticed that Lily suddenly had a faraway look on her face.

Then she said, "Cynthia, after I pass, I want to let people know I'm thinking of them. So when you speak at my funeral, will you tell them …" Lily paused with a dreamy look in her eyes. "Tell them I'll use feathers." She smiled, seeming to remember how powerful the dream of Leah had been. "And I'll use angels and hearts and maybe birds. Yeah, I'll have special birds come around, and they'll know it's me just saying hi and loving them."

I pictured Lily attending her own funeral. "Cynthia, tell them not to be so afraid. It can be better next time." As she spoke, I realized that reflecting on her life was soothing her soul.

"And I hope I loved enough. I hope I passed this time." Lily's expression was wistful. "Remember in one class you said the Dalai Lama says we'll be asked only one question on our deathbed, and it was 'Did I love well?'" I nodded and looked into her blue eyes.

"Cynthia, do you think I've loved well?"

I was shocked that she would ask me this. "Lily, you passed with an A+. You were the best student ever!" I leaned over and kissed her forehead. "You were love itself ... a beautiful soul who taught the world so much."

The day turned into evening, and each of us took turns in the room with Lily. I noticed that Lily was drifting more and more, her breath appearing a little more labored. The nurse kept a close watch on her pain level, giving her occasional injections to ease the pain.

I decided before leaving that I would cancel the next day's appointments and spend the day with her, hoping the family would continue to be comfortable with me there. Lily was like a daughter to me. I could not imagine being anywhere else.

"Cynthia, Do You Think
I Will Go Today?"

It was early the next morning, and Lily had just awakened from her sleep. She was squinting her eyes, and she seemed groggy, her breath shallow. I noticed her chin was trembling. "Cynthia?"

"I'm right here, Lily." I pulled my chair closer to the bed and rested my hand on her hand.

"Is Mason here?" She turned her face toward the door as if she might see him there.

"No, honey. He's not here right now." Lily seemed uneasy, worried. Mason had not returned to see her. He had said he would come by the next day, and it was already two days later.

I spoke softly. "Everything's okay." Lily had started drifting in and out of consciousness. I just wanted to soothe her.

I couldn't get Mason off my mind. I wondered where he was or if he would return. I couldn't ignore my concerns for Lily's desire to be loved by him, yet I felt deep down that he was unreliable. I doubted he would come back. My heart was so heavy.

I thought of the times when she had suffered and when she told me she wanted to belong. I wanted so much to satisfy her every

CYNTHIA LYNCH BISCHOFF, PHD

desire. I wanted to produce Mason for her. I wanted to give her peace. I wanted her to feel loved.

Her family loved her. Her friends loved her. I loved her. But it wasn't the same; I wanted Mason to love her or just be good to her so she felt loved. Did he understand how vulnerable she was, how scared? I didn't know where he was, and Lily seemed to be leaving us quickly.

I spent the morning in and out of her room, reading her more cards and messages, watching her as she slept, noticing that her breathing was becoming harder. Her condition was declining. I wasn't sure how much longer she would hold consciousness.

Later in the morning, she seemed a little more lucid and asked me, "Cynthia, do you think I will go today?"

"I don't know, honey. It might be today. I know you're ready, but it will happen when your soul is ready. We have to trust divine order and timing." Then I added, "I'll be here, just like I said. I promise you I'll be here. I love you."

Her voice seemed a little more urgent, and she said something very clearly that surprised me. "Cynthia, when I get to the other side, what do you want me to do for you?"

I was deeply touched that she would ask me this. "Oh, Lily, you have done so much for me. You don't have to do anything. I just want you to be so joyful when you get there."

Lily cocked her head to the side and seemed to look directly at me. "But maybe I will be able to do something for you, like ask God something for you. I think I'll be able to do that. And I want to help you just like you helped me so much."

I noticed an intensity in her blue eyes, and she seemed to need to hear my answer.

"Well," I said slowly. I realized that she seemed to need to help me too and that, for whatever reason, maybe this was part of her mission. So I continued, "If it is possible for me to help others here, maybe to give them a greater understanding about life and the other side and to help them not to be afraid, like you said I've helped you, well, Lily, maybe you can ask that I have the opportunity to do that."

I paused, trying to word my ideas so she could understand clearly. In my heart, I felt that Lily would go to the other side and ask that very question.

Lily looked up at me and spoke softly. "I promise, Cynthia. I'll ask for that." Her face seemed to radiate as she smiled weakly. Then she closed her eyes, and I felt her focus on her inner world, on her own journey.

I sat for a while holding her hand, studying her dear face, and my heart was full of gratitude and love for this gentle soul. Those were the last words Lily ever spoke to me.

2/

Each Lifetime, Each Pearl, Is an Opportunity to Learn

At noon the next day, Nurse Jody came in and decided to hook Lily up to an oxygen machine. She needed assistance to breathe now. We realized that Lily had entered a semiconscious state. I left the room while she bathed her and changed her clothes, combed her hair.

When I reentered the room, Lily looked beautiful. A long purple dress flowed around her, her hair was braided to one side, her eyes closed, and despite the machine, her breathing had become more labored. In contrast to the previous quiet, the oxygen machine was loud, piercing what had been so still.

Each of us took turns in the room, making sure someone was always present. At one point, I was in the kitchen with Colette, and Jody came in. She had a quizzical look on her face and asked us, "Is it possible there is someone who still needs to be here to say goodbye? ... I've worked in hospice for years, and I know when there is a sense from a patient that something is incomplete."

Colette and I exchanged glances, and the nurse returned to Lily's room to give us space to talk as though she had done her duty.

"Colette, I think I know what's going on with Lily. She's only semiconscious, but I believe people can hear us when we speak with them, no matter what state they're in. I want to reassure her that everything is okay."

"Sure. Go ahead."

I walked back to Lily's room, cracked the door gently, and motioned to Jody that I had a question. We stepped into the hall, and I whispered softly and very briefly to her that there was one possibility of someone who wasn't here, and that it might not be possible for that person to be here. I asked if I could talk to Lily alone about the situation. I asked her if she thought speaking to Lily might help and mentioned that I believed that no matter the state of consciousness, people can hear us.

"Yes, of course," Jody whispered. "I agree. Please go ahead."

I stood in the doorway and glanced about Lily's room. The peacock was still holding vigil. The angels and crystals were floating whimsically in the room, and Lily's beaded necklaces hung on her dresser, creating a magical effect. I felt like Spirit was indeed present with her, and all was in perfect order and timing.

As I stepped through the door, I asked for divine guidance that I might speak to her in such a way that she would understand and her heart would be lifted from any troubles. The crystal in her window caught the light in just the right way as it sprinkled flashes of color about the floor.

Lily lay in her bed, her head tilted to one side, her breathing labored. I pulled over a chair and sat down, taking her hand and holding it very gently. I remembered our first meeting and how she told me she had come to see me primarily for hope. I wanted today, more than ever, to hang her heart on hope, the hope of an understanding that she would gain in the afterlife.

"Lily, sweetheart." I leaned toward her closely and whispered in her ear so that she would hear me clearly over the sound of the machine but also wanting the conversation to be private. "It's Cynthia. I'm right here with you. I'm sending love to you and so glad I can be with you … Lily, your sister and brother are here too, and they love you very much, and wonderful nurses are helping you. You know, Lily, you wanted to know when you might leave, and you may leave soon. There's no doubt you will be so happy when your loved ones come to greet you. I know they're looking forward to seeing you and leading you home. I know they'll lift you and guide you with pure love." I watched her face as I spoke and felt the warmth of her hand. I prayed with all of my heart she could hear me, and I felt deeply that she did.

"Lily, I'm thinking you may be wondering if Mason is here or if he can be here. I thought it would be important to tell you about him. It seems difficult for him to be here right now, but I want you to know he loves you, and he knows you love him. He really wants you to know that he is grateful that he was with you in this lifetime. There's no doubt that you love each other. It may not make sense right now why he's not here, Lily, but I know you will understand fully when you get to the other side." I paused, covering my face for a moment to control my emotions.

I collected myself and continued, my voice shaking, "Remember in classes we said that often we're not clear why something happens the way it does, but we have to trust? And that we know that everything will become clear when we pass?"

I glanced about the room, recalling the tenderest moments of Lily's story as she had shared it with me over the years that I had known her. I continued, trying not to tear up. "Lily, in life, there are so many mysteries, yet we trust that there is a divine plan to it all. So, I want you to know that Mason loves you. I know you will understand everything when you get to the other side, so please don't worry. Everything is okay." I knew in my heart that Mason probably had trouble loving himself, which necessarily makes it difficult to show love fully for someone else.

"Remember, sweetheart, we said that each lifetime, each pearl, is an opportunity to learn. Your soul is eternal, and your learning will continue. Your life is like a tapestry, and on earth we see only the backside, the knotted threads and tangled yarn. Yet at the end of life, the tapestry is turned over, and you will realize that everything contributed to the perfect picture of your life, the perfect way to learn this time."

I looked around the room at the whimsical décor, the angels on the dresser. "You're a beautiful soul, Lily, and you have worked so hard. Soon, this one pearl of your life will be complete ... How important each pearl is! How important you are. Your family loves you so much, and they're taking good care of you. Everyone loves you. Please know that you are always so loved and connected to us."

I continue to hold her hand. I could feel my own heart quieting down as I sent Lily peaceful heart energy. I asked Archangel Gabriel to protect her heart, her tender soul. Then, I rose and went into the hallway to get the nurse. In the kitchen, I told Colette that I had simply explained that everything was well, we were all here, and we loved Lily. Colette thanked me.

An hour later, the nurse came into the kitchen, letting us know that Lily's blood pressure was better. She seemed much more peaceful, and the nurse said that she might last a few more days like this. She wasn't sure. She suggested that I go home if I wanted to. I glanced at Colette and at the nurse and asked if I might stay instead since we didn't know the day or time and I would not break the promise I had given Lily to be with her.

22

"I Think I Stood for Love and for Peace."

The afternoon continued with Andrew, Colette, Nurse Jody, and me taking turns in the room with Lily.

Colette had brought more chairs from the living room into the bedroom so that anyone who wished to be with Lily could stay in the room. I chose a chair toward the far left corner of the bed facing Lily, wanting her family to have the seats nearer to her.

Her brother-in-law, Henry, came by, Colette's husband, and he seemed like a kind man. He had a gentle voice and demeanor, almost a little shy. The three of us, Colette, Andrew, and I, were each sitting in chairs around the bed, and Henry pulled up a chair near us. Each person said something beautiful to Lily, and Henry thanked Lily for being so kind in this lifetime and told her he had written a poem for her. My heart was touched as he recited his poem about love and how she was like love. I knew in her consciousness she could hear him, and I felt that his words were tender and true.

As I watched her caring family embrace Lily in her dying state, I felt privileged to be present, and I realized that what Lily had shared with me earlier was so wise. "Well, I think I stood for love … and for peace. I would tell people not to be so afraid and to make the most of what they can this time."

I realized that as we sat around the bed, we had created a beautiful circle around Lily and that she herself had become the candle, the glowing light in the center, like the light in all the groups in my office that she had found solace in. Lily herself was light.

My mind wandered through thoughts of life, passing, and love as I gazed at her face, her body, her perfection. I watched each breath she took and reflected how in modern science we seek to answer the question of whether there is an afterlife. How often we need proof when, in fact, our intuition, our hearts, our knowing, and our ability to sense and feel life in many dimensions is so vital and real. How often do meaningful coincidences and chance encounters occur beyond our control, while nature offers us omens and signs all the time? How could we doubt divine presence among us?

What is our spirit, our essence? Is our physical body necessary only to help us with lessons in the world of matter? Is a new body in a new lifetime simply a costume to wear as one learns those life lessons? Was Lily's body and even her recurrent cancer the best way to allow her growth and lessons for her soul's understanding this time?

I wondered if it would help people to have an understanding like Lily had achieved about life and the other side so that they could embrace life fully and not die afraid, and I wondered if their loved ones would be comforted by such an awareness of the process of life as well.

I thought of a client whose son had died very suddenly at sixteen in a car accident and how deep her grief was, how I understood her fully when she felt like her life had ended when his did. Over time, she found comfort in believing that his incarnation this time may have been complete, that there were no mistakes, and there was nothing she could have done, even though her mind often wandered through her grief, searching for answers. She felt strongly they would reunite in the afterlife, and she was open to messages and signs that she felt were from him.

Likewise, I knew in my heart that it was critical to understand that what we thought and believed about life and death and about ourselves was essential to living fully. There was such truth in Lily's statement that she had finally found comfort in surrendering and in the power of "not being so afraid of life or of passing."

As the evening wore on, one or two of us at a time would go into the living room to rest, while others remained in the room with Lily, with someone always keeping watch over her.

I sighed as a feeling of growing comfort came over me, bittersweet in knowing deep down that our spirit, our consciousness, does not die with us, but rather it is an integral part of our soul, a part of us that lives on. As Michelangelo[17] said, we are always "still learning"— and I added, yes, *even after we pass.*

I reflected on works I had read and what I had learned abroad, the idea that each soul chooses its own exit point in cooperation with Spirit and an awareness of what is best for its growth in consciousness in that lifetime. I also knew we had free will, and I believed that our choices were powerful in cooperation with divine timing. I fully understood that souls worked together in groups as teachers for one another. Despite this understanding, I also knew that so many challenges, especially tragedies, were so difficult to accept.

I reflected yet again on another client who lost her toddler from heart disease. So many times I had thought, *How could she make sense of this tragedy?* Yet she told me that in praying intensely and reading books about the afterlife, she began to accept that in this lifetime, her child's soul experience was complete. Despite her enormous grief, she learned over time to rest her heart in trusting that they would reunite and that the souls of her child and herself were both learning courageously. My heart could not imagine the grief of losing a small child, and with the deepest humility, I could only honor the soulful work she was doing.

My client had told me that with the deep love and care that she and her family had given her child, the child had been a teacher

---

[17] "Michelangelo," Wikiquote, accessed March 17, 2019, https://en.wikiquote.org/wiki/Michelangelo.

who contributed to the soulful growth of the family itself, of her soul group. She knew her love for her son would never die and that their souls would live on, that one day the family would reunite on the other side, and that all would be understood. She told me that rather than take away the pain of loss, her growing awareness had become a balm to calm her heart.

All these stories I had experienced with dear clients in their state of loss, yet still I struggled to make sense of the loss of Lily. Here was one life story that meant more to me than any other because the bond Lily and I shared was so full of genuine love.

I closed my eyes and sent loving hope to Lily. I thought of her sweet and gentle nature, of how long she had suffered and how frightened she had been in this lifetime about dying. I imagined her as a newborn baby, sweet in her mother's arms, remembering how close she said they had been. I knew without doubt that she would reunite with her mother in the afterlife and be greeted again by her loving embrace.

23

We Will Surely Meet Again

As it nears eleven o'clock at night, I hear the front door open. I am sitting at the bedside with Jody and Lily's family. Jody leaves the room to go into the kitchen. I hear her exchange greetings for a few minutes with the nurse who has come to relieve her.

Moments later, a woman with short, dark hair pokes her head into the bedroom door. She has a sweet look about her, a smile that seems earthy, like someone who would enjoy a beautiful sunset and care deeply to help her patient, a person who seems as gentle as Lily herself. She smiles at Colette, Andrew, and me as she enters the room.

The lamp in the corner is casting a calm light onto Lily's bed. The new nurse, Helena, speaks softly as she introduces herself, telling us that she has worked in hospice for many years and is glad to be here to help us. After reading over the notes, she examines Lily carefully, assessing what seems to me to be more than just the physical realm. She takes Colette aside, and I hear her ask if it would be okay to take Lily off the oxygen machine. She's concerned that the loud noise it makes is more disturbing than helpful at this point, and that while she is not sure if Lily will pass soon or in a day or so, she feels that the machine might interfere with the natural progression of her passing. And so with agreement, she turns off the machine and, with Andrew's help, moves it into the hall. Instantly there is a distinct sense of peace in the room. Helena's proficiency is second nature; it lends us a bit of confidence in the midst of our helplessness.

Helena whispers softly, asking me how I know Lily and to tell her something about what Lily loved in this lifetime. I share that Lily loved her plants and animals and, of course, her family and especially those loved ones who had passed on, and so she asks me if I might help bring some of the plants and pictures from the front room into the bedroom.

As I gather things, I notice what great care Lily has given to her beloved possessions, especially a beautiful prayer plant that caught my eye. Once in the bedroom, Helena and I work together to place items on the bedside tables, the plants along with pictures of her family. I notice that the nurse is placing the grandmother's picture next to a plaque I gave Lily, a small wooden circle with a bird etched into the wood, a plaque about her being so very brave.

I reflect on the moment I bought that plaque for her. It was early on when I had met her, and she was struggling to maintain the courage to attempt healing from a second bout of cancer. It touches me that she kept it all these years and even more that she was, indeed, so brave.

The nurse suggests that some soft music might be nice, and I think of the music that I play at the end of each Heartliving class, knowing that Lily will be familiar with it and may find it comforting. The CD is in her collection. Soon, the soft music is playing in the background.

We light the votive candles on the dresser and mantel to enhance the calming light of the soft lamp. Helena reaches into a backpack that she brought and pulls out rose lotion. Gently, she moves the cover off Lily's feet and rubs lotion on her feet and legs, massaging her gently until the room smells of roses. She props her with pillows on either side so that she is sure Lily is comfortable. I feel as though Spirit has sent her here.

The clock now chimes midnight. We look at one another. Colette is exhausted and has been up for hours. She whispers that she will lie down in the living room on the couch for a bit, and Andrew agrees to summon her if we think Lily is passing.

I'm clear that I am now aware of two dimensions—the physical realm in which we are present with Lily's physical body and the spiritual awareness that her spirit will transition soon into a new dimension. I see Lily lying majestically in the center of her four-poster bed, her long purple dress flowing around her, her hair braided to one side. Her breath is becoming more and more labored, yet her face and body seem serene and expectant.

I glance about the room at Lily's personal treasures here in her sanctuary, the books, journals, crystals, necklaces, and alabaster angels, all of which meant so much to her in this lifetime. I realize that many physical things sustain us while we are on earth. Each carries a meaning, a vibration. All contribute to our learning, whether they offer us a sense of peace or distraction. Yet it is our spirit, our consciousness, that we take with us as we transition into a new realm. I reflect on how often we don't give our consciousness the attention that we give the earthly things. I am so grateful that Lily valued learning, that when she embraced her eventual passing, she looked forward to going back to her "spiritual home," as she told me.

I take a deep breath and look down at my own hands, aware that I am aging in my physical body but that, like Lily, I am comfortable in my spiritual consciousness, more wedded to my internal than external world. Perhaps the many times I had to let go of physical comforts for one reason or another, to encounter people leaving my life and me leaving theirs, it was these experiences that caused me to look within my heart and to find my meaning there. I remembered the wisdom of Dr. Jung's words: "He who looks outside dreams. He who looks inside awakens."[18]

18 "Carl Gustav Jung," Quotation Reference, accessed March 17, 2019, http://www.quotationreference.com/quotefinder.php?strt=1&subj= Carl+Gustav+Jung&byax=1&lr=.

I also know that, like Lily, I value all the experiences of my life, or as Dr. Jung so wisely put it, "Even a happy life cannot be without a measure of darkness, and the word 'happy' would lose its meaning if it were not balanced by sadness."[19] I know that all experiences and challenges have contributed to the entirety of Lily's learning.

I know that dying is simply an ending of one's physical body but not of one's spirit, an ending simply of the physical container that houses the spirit, and I am aware that after our passing, our spirit moves into another dimension. We, the living, are no longer able to see the person without the physical body, so we experience what we call the "death" of the person, and certainly it is the death of their physical body only. Their spirit is eternal.

The time passes into this dark night as Andrew, Helena, and I hold presence for Lily's soul. There has become a dreaminess about the room, a feeling of vibration and peace, yet a sense of pregnant expectation. From time to time, I notice Lily's cat staring at me as she scratches on the floor in the corner.

I close my eyes, and my mind starts wandering through a review of my times with Lily, so many sacred moments together, so many conversations about life. I remember Lily asking me early on if our souls ever die. "Cynthia, does the soul simply take up residence in a physical body each lifetime? Is there an end to lifetimes at some point, and if so, what happens to the soul then?"

We reflected together on the idea that the soul's evolution will take place through the learnings of many lifetimes and that each individual soul may operate at a different pace than another, with each soul helping the other. Lily had reflected on how she had met certain people with whom she felt a magnetic draw and that she knew their souls recognized each other from another time. She told me she once had a friend whom she felt she had known forever. We decided that as we travel through lifetimes with our soul groups, there are souls we have known many lifetimes before, and, yes, we will have feelings as though we have known them forever.

---

[19] "Carl Jung Quotes," Brainy Quote, accessed March 17, 2019, https://www.brainyquote.com/quotes/carl_jung_157285.

I knew that her connections to the hearts of others and our conversations about the other side, our pondering the challenging questions of life after passing, were perhaps the most important moments of Lily's last year. She needed to know what her mission had been and to understand the contribution she had made—the spiritual gifts that had emerged in her in this lifetime, her loving nature as well as her need for peace and harmony. She needed to be clear about the legacy she was leaving behind. "Cynthia, what did I stand for? Did I pass in this lifetime?"

She was comforted by the dream of her grandmother, who told her she would not be judged but rather would look gently at what she had learned. Lily had remarked, "Grandmother said it's all about love."

I realize that I am drifting in and out of consciousness. Suddenly, I hear a stir in the room and open my eyes fully to notice that Helena is checking Lily's vitals, swabbing her lips to keep her mouth moist. She glances at Andrew and me, then pulls her chair a little closer to Lily, whose breath has become raspier and more congested, more of a rattling sound with a shortness in between breaths.

Suddenly I am aware of what appears to be a blue crystal image at the center of Lily's heart. I focus on the image and notice that it seems to pulsate. Images are appearing within the crystal, but it is difficult for me to distinguish them. I feel I am floating in between worlds with her. I close my eyes and open them, the blue crystal intensifying in my vision. The nightstands around the bed appear to be vibrating now with a kind of in-and-out motion, feeling like they are composed of waves of energy.

As I feel more and more in spirit myself, I whisper to Lily through my consciousness, "Lily, we are here, and we love you dearly. We admire how brave you have been for so long. We are so grateful for you. You have taught us so much. You will soon be guided into the beautiful dimension that your grandmother described. She will come for you."

It is as though her grandmother in the picture near the bed is looking now directly at me with a knowingness as the frame sways in vibration. Suddenly, her grandmother in the picture has become three-dimensional although transparent. She is no longer bound to the frame, and Lily is no longer bound to her body. The two spirits are embracing.

I see white light enveloping Lily and her grandmother. Their images are merging, and the light becomes brighter. It fills my heart and takes my breath away.

Helena now glances at Andrew and me. She nods yes for Andrew to go get Colette. Andrew leaves the room quickly, and just as he returns to the bedroom, followed by Colette, a chime is heard in the room, fully audible but from no earthly source. We look at one another in wonder, and it is clear that we have all heard it. We realize Lily has taken her last breath. Helena nods her head to confirm this as she checks Lily's vitals. Then, Helena leans toward us and whispers, "Often, a sound is heard as a person passes."

We are all standing now around the bed, looking down at Lily. Colette and Andrew have embraced each other. Helena and I move into the kitchen, giving Colette and Andrew time to say goodbye to their sister. In the kitchen, Helena and I hug each other, and she remarks that she has never known a patient like Lily, whose hands remained so warm, even at her death. Lily, she said, was truly special.

Soon Colette and Andrew enter the kitchen, and I am given time alone to say goodbye to Lily. I walk into the bedroom, which is now quiet and still. I am stunned at how beautiful Lily is, at her glowing skin. Her peace is palpable. I kneel by her bed and take her warm hands in mine and speak to her from the bottom of my heart, letting her know I love her and that our hearts will be forever joined.

Tears fill my eyes, and I pause in silence as our hearts speak. I know that our connection is not over, that we will communicate, and that we will surely meet again. I turn to leave the room, then stand at the door and look back again at Lily, seeing her in all her majesty in both dimensions, capturing her image forever in my heart.

I Keep Vigil over My Own Soul

As I enter the kitchen, Colette, Andrew, and Helena are discussing the specifics of calling the coroner and funeral home to pick up Lily's body, filling out the proper paperwork. I know that I need to leave them to this private work. I feel so awkward. I don't want to be a burden, yet my heart doesn't want to leave Lily.

Colette suddenly goes into the living room and comes back with a picture of me that Lily had framed. She hands it to me. "Thank you, Cynthia. We appreciate all you have done." I hug Colette and clutch my picture to my heart. It is time for me to leave.

I put my coat on and open the door to leave. Once I enter the dimly lit hallway, I can see the darkness outside through the upper-story window, a tree branch swaying. I glance at my watch and realize that it is after three in the morning. A shiver comes over me as I enter the bitter cold air, bringing me back into my physical body. I grasp the picture again close to my heart as I make my way down the stairs.

As I leave the building, I look up and down the dark street. I feel so alone and emotionally distraught that I walk with a bit of a stagger as I make my way to my car. I am going home to an empty house. My heart is so heavy. I want to cry hysterically, to release the energy of weeks of fear.

Once inside the car, I sob uncontrollably, my head on the steering wheel. Yet the darkness around me makes me gather myself up and drive numbly home. I know the Heartliving book club will meet at eight o'clock in the morning, and I told the group weeks before that if I could not be there, I would call a member very early who would let the others know. This is the book club that Lily had been in. *I will not cancel*, I thought. *I will go to the group and share Lily's passing with them.*

I drive cautiously, not feeling grounded in my body. Once home, I cannot sleep, feeling weeks of fear and sadness come up. I cannot enter the bedroom. It is as though I cannot focus. I collapse into an overstuffed chair in my den, crying endlessly as I stare through tears into the burning gas logs in the fireplace. I vacillate between saying in my mind, "Lily, you're home! I know you're so happy!" to thoughts of "Lily, my God, I miss you so much." I keep vigil over my own soul.

In a couple of short hours, I take a shower and dress, gathering my books and materials for the book club. The world has taken on a surreal feeling. I am in the world but not feeling of it.

Once I am at my office, participants start arriving. The first asks about Lily, and we both hug and cry. Soon others arrive with a knowing at first glance, and all of us hug one another. We sit together in our circle, and I share the story of Lily's passing, her beautiful questions, her courage, how she plans to let them know she's near. We share loving stories of her, certain memories, how we thought she was an earth angel, a fairy perhaps. We end our session by holding hands in the circle, candle in the center as always, placing her spirit in the middle of the group, sending her love while feeling her peace.

After class, I decide to cancel the remaining appointments for the day, knowing I will be unable to function. I lie on the office couch and try to relax. I find myself reminiscing about Lily, our time together, and where her spirit may be now. I remember the day I met her and she gave me daffodils. Her blue eyes so intense, her spirit so gentle, her desires so great.

I fall asleep for several hours and am awakened abruptly by the phone.

"Hello?"

"Cynthia? This is Mason. Can you talk?"

I am startled to hear from him but answer, "Yes, Mason."

"How's Lily?" Mason speaks slowly, and then there is a pause. "Is she okay?"

"Mason, this is so hard to tell you," I say slowly, hesitating, "but Lily passed away early this morning." As much as I wish he'd been there for her, I do not feel I can judge his circumstances.

There is silence on his end, and then he says with a sincere and soft voice, "I thought she did, Cynthia. I really thought she'd passed. You know, I was in my car early this morning, and while I was driving, a seagull swooped down and flew directly in front of my windshield. I felt like it was Lily telling me she was free. You know, she always said the seagull was her animal."

"Oh, Mason. I bet it was her way of letting you know."

"You know, I wanted to be there." Mason hesitates and then continues, "I mean I've done some stuff and all. But I wanted to be there." There is silence again. "Lily knows I loved her. I thought about her the whole time. I'm glad she's free now." I could hear his voice breaking up.

"Mason, I told Lily that you loved her. It calmed her down to know that ... and, Mason, she loved you too. She was grateful for her time with you." I realize not only can I not judge Mason, but I also have to trust that everything has worked out as it was supposed to. Lily would understand on the other side.

Mason hesitates and then speaks up. "Thank you. I'm glad she's out of pain."

"Mason, if you want to talk about anything, you can call me. Okay? Remember, I told Lily I'd do that."

"Okay," he said quietly. "Cynthia, is there going to be a service?"

"I know there will be a service, but I don't know when yet."

As a start to fulfilling my promise to Lily to help Mason, I decide to go one step further and tell him, "Some of the women in our book club talked about having a small gathering at my office this week on Friday evening at seven to light candles and just remember her. You are welcome if you'd like to come to that gathering."

"Cynthia, I know where your office is. I'll be there."

"Good. I'll see you then."

We hang up, and although I know nothing of his beliefs and am sad that he was not there, particularly sad for Lily, I feel moved that Mason seemed tuned into Lily in a completely different dimension.

25

May You Rejoice in Your New Life, Free of Pain and Suffering

That night, I lay in my bed, my heart restless, recalling every moment of Lily's passing. I thought deeply about her, wondering how her spirit was. I was so glad that her grandmother had come for her. I had no doubt that she was happy and glad to see her loved ones and her animals when she arrived on the other side. I wondered if she was "cocooned" for a while, as we had learned about—that is, whether she was kept in a healing state to allow her to receive care and love, just a gentle holding as she adjusted to the new dimension.

I thought of my life, how I had left a secure job years before to create my Heartliving work, how my desire for growth in my inner world had always dominated my outer need for security. I wondered how much longer I had in this incarnation, how many lessons I might still learn.

My mind was a kaleidoscope of thoughts and feelings, a myriad of emotions. I felt so fragile. I gazed at the moonlight shining through the top of the bedroom window, casting light on my sanctuary—my books, icons, and watercolor paintings. I had purchased two silk scarves, both the same, the two angels, one silk scarf for Lily and one for me. I had framed mine, the light hitting it just right on this evening, showing the two angels holding hands, floating ever so gently. "Thank you, Lily," I whispered. "I love that we held hands in this lifetime. May you rejoice in your new life, free of pain and suffering."

I drifted off to sleep, and when I awoke to my phone ringing in the early morning, I felt how stiff and sore my body was, as though I had been involved in deep physical work. *It's amazing*, I thought, *how the body mirrors the mind and spirit.*

I was surprised that Colette was calling so early. She mentioned that Lily had wanted me to speak at her funeral, to do the eulogy, and she wondered if I would be okay with that. She told me they would have a minister too but hoped that I could say a few words about Lily. I told her that I would be honored to do that.

Colette proceeded to give me the details of the funeral. There would be a graveside service where I would speak along with the minister, followed by a reception at a museum with beautiful gardens that Lily had loved. There would be no microphone, but she hoped people would gather closely to hear since it would be outdoors and probably very cold.

"Yes, Colette. I can do that. We will make it beautiful for Lily. Once I get the details of Lily's service from you, I'll send them along to her friends, especially those she knew through my work, and I'll make sure they tell others as well."

"Thanks, Cynthia. Her obituary will be in tomorrow's paper, and the details will be in it." She paused. "Thanks and take good care. I'll see you then."

"You too, Colette."

I will begin writing the eulogy today, I thought. I curled up in a chair with my notebook and pen. There was so much I wanted to say about Lily. It seemed at first that the ideas were flowing, yet I would intermittently find myself crying as I imagined standing in the graveyard and Lily looking down on all of us there. I wrote, then cried, then wrote again. Finally, I had written enough of a draft to put it aside, knowing that I could read it again tomorrow and continue reflecting and writing until I felt completely comfortable that Lily was honored in the way that I had hoped she would be.

It was December, and as I went outside to put food in the bird feeder, I realized how cold it had become. *It will be so cold in the graveyard*, I thought. *Dress warmly so you can speak without shivering, without crying, with your voice strong to give Lily's message.*

I remembered a conversation I'd had with Lily once. She loved working as a master gardener, and I had shared some quotes I'd heard about planting, about gardens, and about life. A Thomas Merton quote was a favorite of hers: "Every moment and every event of our lives on earth plants something in our soul."[20] She told me she had no doubt about the truth of that statement.

In my teaching of literature, a quote by Robert Louis Stevenson had also moved me, so I had shared it with Lily, "Don't judge each day by the harvest you reap but by the seeds that you plant."[21] I thought of the seeds that Lily had planted in my heart and in the hearts of so many.

I also knew how much Lily loved birds, how feathers were one of her signs, so I glanced at the beautiful words of poets such as Emily Dickinson, William Wordsworth, Rainer Maria Rilke, and Langston Hughes, among others.

I wrote and rewrote the eulogy, added and removed quotes, read and reread it out loud, until on the eighth practice attempt, I could read it without crying. I was satisfied that Lily would be honored in the way that she deserved. Finally, a calmness came over me.

---

[20] "Thomas Merton Quotes> Quotes > Quotable Quotes," Goodreads, accessed March 17, 2019, https://www.goodreads.com/quotes/705087-every-moment-and-every-event-of-every-man-s-life-on.
[21] "Robert Louis Stevenson Quotes," Brainy Quote, accessed March 17, 2019, https://www.brainyquote.com/quotes/robert_louis_stevenson_101230.

26

We All Agreed What an Earth Angel Lily Had Been

The day of Lily's memorial gathering at my office arrived, and although we had decided to limit the gathering to those who knew her through class, with their permission, I asked if Mason could attend, and they were fine with that. I felt Lily would be present in spirit, and I wanted Mason to have another opportunity to show up for her.

I arrived early at the office that evening and placed the bowl on the table, complete with votive candles as Lily had done previously for Pop. Everyone was familiar with my office and our rituals, such as meditation, and I was hoping that Mason would feel comfortable.

People began to gather and take a seat. It was nearing seven o'clock, and Mason knocked at the door. He was dressed in neatly pressed khaki pants and a pin-striped shirt, his hair was well combed, and I was surprised at how different he looked. I noticed he was holding an envelope and a box of candy. He glanced around the room. "Lily told me her groups had mostly women in them, so I thought you'd all like some candy. I got copies of a picture of Lily too, so you could each have one." He placed the candy on the table and opened the envelope and took out four-by-six copies of a picture of Lily, handing one to each of us.

I looked down at the picture and was immediately filled with emotion. I saw our radiant Lily standing outdoors. The sunlight was hitting her shoulder-length blonde hair and illuminating her face and bright blue eyes. Her smile was broad, and her head cocked to one side. She wore a long yellow dress, embroidered with flowers of china blue, orange, and red that seemed to float down the river of her body. Her dress was gathered at the waist with a wide leather belt, a golden color that matched her hair. In the center of the belt was a circle with decorative beads in the shape of a sunflower. Lily was standing proudly next to the lion cage at the zoo. I remembered her telling us how often she loved to visit the animals there.

This lion was familiar to me. In the early-summer sunlight, like Lily, he was golden. He sat upright, his thick mane falling around his face like a being in deep sleep. His giant paws were crossed. He was powerful yet gentle.

I was overcome with emotion as I remembered the many times in childhood I had visually drawn him on the wall next to my bed. There was silence as tears fell down my cheeks, and I covered my face with my hands. I reached for a tissue, then wiped my eyes and looked back at the group. Jaeda and Courtney were sitting on either side of me. Each reached over and took one of my hands. They did not let go of them. I tried to contain myself, choking back my emotion. We went around the circle, and each person spoke about Lily and lit a candle in her honor.

When it was Mason's turn, he looked down when he spoke. His hands were clasped around a picture of Lily, and his fingers nervously bent the edges. He told us how sweet and strong Lily was, how sorry he was that she had to pass, and that she had taught him a lot. Then he said something that was surprising and very moving. He confided that his younger sister had died the year before of breast cancer. Mason told us that he hoped Lily and his sister might be together.

Candice reached for the tissue box, passed it around the circle, and we all dabbed our eyes as we watched Mason light a candle in Lily's honor. I knew that Lily was watching.

27

Your Memory Will Live in Our Hearts Forever

My alarm woke me from a deep sleep. It was very early on Saturday, the morning of Lily's service. I checked the weather, and the temperature was below freezing. I stumbled out of bed, showered, and began dressing warmly, pulling on a leotard and long skirt, tights, socks, and boots. I draped a thick cape around my shoulders and put on a dark purple hat, gathering up my notes for the eulogy.

As I arrived at the graveyard very early, the attendant told me the exact plot where Lily was to be buried. The graveyard seemed immense. As I drove to the back of the lot, I passed gravestones, some covered with fresh flowers and some with dried wreaths, stones on which statues of angels and crosses stood proudly. I thought of how tenuous life is.

I reached the back of the lot, parked the car, and sat for a few moments, the first one to arrive. A small tent was already in place, covering the spot where Lily's tribute would take place.

I felt sensitized to every movement around me, noticing the crisp winter air, the fallen leaves. The sky was clear, and soft clouds spaciously present. I saw various birds perched on trees and flying about. I knew that Lily was to be buried next to her parents, and

I remembered being at the graveyard a few years before when I had accompanied her to her mother's funeral. The area her family had chosen for their plots was picturesque, with large trees draping branches over gravestones.

I took a deep breath and sat in the car staring out the window at the graveyard plots in an expanse of land devoted to so many loved ones. The sky was gray, but a tiny bit of light shone through onto the dash. I could see in the distance an elderly man standing at a grave. He wore a long, thick winter coat and a black fedora. He knelt down and bowed his head, and I noticed that he held a book that he seemed to be reading from. I hoped that he had found peace and that his loved one was looking over him somewhere not too far from his reach.

Suddenly, my heart began to race with a mix of grief and anticipation. My mind was a myriad of emotion. I thought of Lily, how innocent yet wise she was, how much she had gone through, how precious our lives are. I thought of how we cannot predict our journey, how we go through life often wondering why we are here, what our purpose is, and whether we are fulfilling it.

I thought of my own life, of how much richer my life had become with Lily having been a part of it, but, oh, how this existence I'd chosen could at times break my heart. I knew it was my calling and privilege to help others through their worry, tragedy, suffering, but even more important, their solutions and growth. Still, their circumstances and misfortune weighed heavily on me at times.

I am not in a loving partnership, and my children have both finished college and moved away. There is a natural, healthy progression in their lives of creating their own families. I am so proud of all they are becoming, and I treasure every moment I spend with them.

I reminded myself that I am in this world but not always feeling of it. Like Lily described, I have not always fit in by outer standards, but I have remained true to the absolutely binding inner law of my own to love through everything.

I opened the car door, pulled my cape tightly around me, pulled my hat down, and walked toward the tent area, past the bare trees and brown grass. I stood off to the side, and soon I saw one person arrive, then another. I watched as Candice, Jaeda, Courtney, Faye, Elaine, and Patricia arrived. Then Evelyn, Asa, Tina, Giulia, Diane, Karen, Marie, Raven, Marva, and other heart sisters. My heart was so full. They walked over and stood with me under an old magnolia tree with its gnarly roots jutted up out of the ground around its trunk. The cold air caused us to huddle together.

Lily's family arrived. Colette came over, and we hugged. Her blue eyes seemed glazed over, and her face drawn. I tried not to cry as her eyes met mine. The family sat together under the small tent, adjacent to Lily's purple urn. More than one hundred people gathered to pay tribute to Lily and her family.

The minister spoke first and said a few words about Lily's life, how much her family loved her, about how dust we are and to dust we shall return. I focused on her family and was numb while listening, praying that I would not cry and that I could speak loudly enough to be heard, to honor Lily as I had promised her, to tell them what she stood for and who she was. Just as I had told her I would.

And so I walked up when the minister motioned to me. I took a deep breath and looked out at the sea of faces, and I began.

"We gather today to pay tribute to our dear friend and loved one Lily. Before she passed, she asked me to speak to you about her life and about what she stood for, to give you her message. I am honored to have that privilege.

"So often it is that a person's life is recorded simply through hospital records and other documentation. These records and the events on which they are based do not address the person to whom certain life events have happened, nor the way in which that special soul gave her gift. And so it is that I will share with you a few ways in which Lily's heart touched the world.

"We all know that Lily's life was not easy. She experienced the challenge of cancer three times and the onset at such a young age. Each time, she tried to do her best to work through her fears. Each time, she remained hopeful, perhaps at first for a cure, but as time went on, hopeful for an understanding about life.

"Through her long experience with illness, she knew that we only borrow these bodies for a short time and that every day is a privilege and opportunity to do our best. And Lily did just that. She was a special person who had the gentlest soul. She was not quick to anger or to judge but rather was sensitive and kind, without judgment or malice toward anyone or anything.

"Lily knew that we participate in each other's lives in powerful ways. She was so grateful for her deeply loving family and dear, kindhearted friends. She said she was at peace with life and complete with everyone.

"She told me once that she remembered something she had heard, that at the end of our lives, we will be asked only one question, and that question was 'Did I love well?' And so Lily asked me that day, 'Cynthia, you know me. Do you think I loved well?' Those of us who knew Lily knew that she was indeed love itself. And I told her just that.

"Lily was a joy to so many people and gave so freely of her love. When she asked me to speak to you, she said, 'Cynthia, please give them this message.' And after careful thought, she said, 'Tell them to love nature, animals, children, and most of all, each other.' She also told me to tell you that if she could, she would give you messages from above, that she would use images of hearts, birds, feathers, and angels as ways to let you know that she was thinking of you.

"She asked me to share with you a beautiful quote she had heard: 'The gown we leave in has no pockets. You can take only what you have in your heart.' We know her heart was full of the love she shared with each of us and the wisdom she gained from her courageous lifetime.

"Lily was so young. We often question why someone so young and kind must be taken. Yet we must trust in the divine who has plans for all of us. No doubt each of us has experienced life events that have occurred in mysterious ways, and we know that often it is only after our lives are over that we will know the reason why things happen the way they do.

"As I stand here today, I reflect on how, like Lily, each of us is born into this world without awareness of what the journey may bring. And how we attempt to make sense of life's incongruities, of life's pain. I think of how Lily experienced such difficult lessons, yet how she triumphed with beauty and dignity. I remember her telling me that it wasn't until she was no longer afraid of dying that she could allow herself to really live. Lily was indeed our teacher.

"And so I believe she would tell you to be mindful, to practice moments of gratitude, and to value quiet time in which you can go inside and know your heart. You see, it is in your own heart that you can come truly to know the world.

"Dearest Lily, you have graced our lives. We will never forget you, for you belong to us and to the world. Your memory will live in our hearts forever."

As I uttered these last words, I paused and closed my eyes, feeling her spirit there among us. My heart was full and heavy with emotion. The graveyard had become so quiet.

Suddenly, breaking the stillness, a cacophony of bird chatter broke out. We all looked up at the large magnolia overhead with its thick branches. A flock of birds had gathered there to sing.

I immediately thought of Lily telling me, "Cynthia, will you tell them? I'll have special birds come around, and they'll know it's me just saying hi and loving them. I mean Pop was a cardinal, and I guess I'll be a bluebird or a seagull or maybe just any bird, and they'll know it's me."

The truth of a poem by Rainer Maria Rilke came to me: "A birdsong can even, for a moment, make the whole world into a sky within us, because we feel that the bird does not distinguish between its heart and the world's."[22]

This, I believe, was true of Lily's heart.

---

[22] Rainer Maria Rilke, *The Inner Sky: Poems, Notes, Dreams, trans.* Damion Searls (Boston: David R. Godine, Publisher, 2010), 117.

References

Andrews, Ted. *Animal-Speak Pocket Guide.* Jackson, TN: Dragonhawk Publishing, 2009.

Bischoff, Cynthia Lynch. Heartliving Guidance Cards. Word-of-the-Day featured daily on Facebook, copyright 2009. https://www.facebook.com/Heartliving.

Brainy Quote. "Carl Jung Quotes." Accessed March 17, 2019. https://www.brainyquote.com/quotes/carl_jung_157285.

Brainy Quote. "Robert Louis Stevenson Quotes." Accessed March 17, 2019. https://www.brainyquote.com/quotes/robert_louis_stevenson_101230.

Childre, Doc, Howard Martin, and Donna Beech. *The HeartMath Solution: The Institute of HeartMath's Revolutionary Program for Engaging the Power of the Heart's Intelligence.* New York: HarperCollins Publishers, 1999.

Groban, Josh. "You Raise Me Up!" YouTube. Accessed March 15, 2019. https://www.youtube.com/watch?v=aJxrX42WcjQ.

Goodreads. "Anais Nin > Quotes > Quotable Quotes." Accessed March 12, 2019. https://www.goodreads.com/quotes/876911-and-the-day-came-when-the-risk-to-remain-tight.

Goodreads. "Thomas Merton > Quotes > Quotable Quotes." Accessed March 17, 2019. https://www.goodreads.com/quotes/705087-every-moment-and-every-event-of-every-man-s-life-on.

Goodreads. "Wayne W. Dyer > Quotes > Quotable Quotes." Accessed March 18, 2019. https://www.goodreads.com/

quotes/30189-with-everything-that-has-happened-to-you-you-
can-either.

International Association of Reiki Professionals. "Learn about Reiki,
Definition of Reiki." Accessed March 17, 2019. https://iarp.org/
learn-about-reiki/.

Joy, W. Brugh. *Joy's Way: A Map for the Transformational Journey: An
Introduction to the Potentials for Healing with Body Energies.* New
York: Putnam, 1979.

Mipon Anime Tourism. "Which Anime is Popular Right Now
in Japan?" Accessed October 5, 2019. https://mipon.org/
anime-popular-right-now-japan/.

Newton, Michael. *Destiny of Souls: New Case Studies of Life between
Lives.* St. Paul, Minnesota: Llewellyn Publications, 2001.

Newton, Michael. *Journey of Souls: Case Studies of Life between Lives.*
St. Paul, Minnesota: Llewellyn Publications, 2003.

Ornish, Dean. *Love and Survival: 8 Pathways to Intimacy and Health.*
New York: HarperCollins Publishers, 1998.

Poetry Foundation. "Star Light, Star Bright." Accessed March
17, 2019. https://www.poetryfoundation.org/poems/46976/
star-light-star-bright.

Quotation Reference. "Carl Gustav Jung." Accessed March
17, 2019. http://www.quotationreference.com/quotefinder.
php?strt=1&subj=Carl+Gustav+Jung&byax=1&lr=.

Rilke, Rainer Maria. *The Inner Sky: Poems, Notes, Dreams by Rainer
Maria Rilke.* Selected and translated by Damion Searls. Boston:
David R. Godine, 2010.

Rilke, Rainer Maria. *Rilke's Book of Hours: Love Poems to God.*
Translated by Anita Barrows and Joanna Macy. New York:
Riverhead Books, 1996.

ScienceDirect. "Energy Healing." Accessed October 5, 2019.
https://www.sciencedirect.com/topics/medicine-and-dentistry/
energy-healing.

Stands4Network. "Definitions, Randoseru." Accessed October 5,
2019. https://www.definitions.net/definition/randoseru.

Taiken Japan. "Morning Exercise in Japan." Accessed October 5, 2019. https://taiken.co/single/morning-exercise/.

US Department of Health and Human Services. "End of Life: What Are Palliative Care and Hospice Care?" NIH > National Institute on Aging. Accessed March 17, 2019. https://www.nia.nih.gov/health/what-are-palliative-care-and-hospice-care#hospice.

Weiss, Brian. *Many Lives, Many Masters: The True Story of a Prominent Psychiatrist, His Young Patient, and the Past Life Therapy that Changed Both Their Lives.* New York: Simon & Schuster, 1988.

Wikipedia. "Avon Products." Accessed October 5, 2019. https://simple.wikipedia.org/wiki/Avon_Products.

Wikiquote. "Michelangelo." Accessed March 17, 2019. https://en.wikiquote.org/wiki/Michelangelo.

Wikiquote. "Ralph Waldo Emerson." Accessed June 19, 2019. https://en.wikiquote.org/wiki/Ralph_Waldo_Emerson.

About the Author

Dr. Cynthia Lynch Bischoff is an international life coach, healing practitioner, and inspirational speaker who teaches and performs sessions in the US, Europe, and Japan. She is the founder of Heartliving—her coaching and seminar business—through which she has delivered holistic coaching and energy-healing sessions, seminars, and products to thousands internationally.

A master speaker and storyteller, Cynthia inspires others through her poignant life journey of risk-taking and living her soul's mission. What distinguishes Cynthia is an authentic compassion and tireless commitment to help walk people through significant, transformational life events. She has helped clients with the most challenging circumstances, such as reframing traumas, managing life-threatening illnesses, and guiding people to understand their life journeys.

Cynthia's unique curriculum is grounded in both business and intuitive principles. Her passion is to assist you in your transformation process.

Currently, Cynthia can be found through the following channels:

US website: www.heartliving.com
Japanese website: http://r.goope.jp/nhsnijinohane
Facebook: www.facebook.com/Heartliving
LinkedIn: www.linkedin.com/in/cynthialbischoff
YouTube channel: HeartlivingVideo

Made in the USA
Middletown, DE
30 November 2021

53826221R00111